Renaissance
Papers
2015

Renaissance Papers 2015

Editors
Jim Pearce and Ward J. Risvold

Assistant Editors
Nathan Dixon and Barry Shelton

❧

Published for
THE SOUTHEASTERN RENAISSANCE CONFERENCE
by
Camden House
Rochester, New York

THE SOUTHEASTERN RENAISSANCE CONFERENCE

2015 Officers

President: Susan Staub, Appalachian State University
Secretary-Treasurer: Emily Stockard, Florida Atlantic University

Renaissance Papers, 2015

Copyright © 2016
The Southeastern Renaissance Conference

ISSN: 0584-4207
ISBN-13: 978-1-57113-964-1
ISBN-10: 1-57113-964-8

Published by:

Camden House
An imprint of Boydell & Brewer, Inc.
668 Mt. Hope Avenue, Rochester, NY 14620-2731, USA
www.camden-house.com

and of Boydell & Brewer Ltd.
P.O. Box 9, Woodbridge, Suffolk IP12 3DF, UK
www.boydellandbrewer.com

CONTENTS

Renaissance Papers

A Selection of Papers
Submitted to the
Seventy-Second Annual Meeting
October 2–3, 2015
University of North Carolina-Chapel Hill
Chapel Hill, North Carolina

The Stuart Brothers and English Theater

David M. Bergeron

THE Herbert brothers, William (Earl of Pembroke) and Philip (Earl of Montgomery), achieved immortality through the dedication of the Shakespeare Folio to them in 1623. All the Folios through the seventeenth century continued to carry the identical dedication even though the brothers had since died, which makes the whole enterprise a little strange.[1] In contrast, the Stuart brothers Ludovic (1574–1624) and Esmé (1579–1624) enjoyed no such fate and fame, yet their influence at the Jacobean court and in the arts rivals the better-known duo. The failure of the *Oxford Dictionary of National Biography* to pay any attention to the Stuart brothers' support of the arts has spurred my quest. The brothers' father, also named Esmé, was a French first cousin to King James's father, Henry Stuart, Earl of Darnley. As long as James was childless, Ludovic stood in immediate line of succession to the Scottish throne, as James dutifully noted. My research reveals details of the brothers' involvement with drama and underscores the multifaceted nature of patronage in Stuart England.

The brothers' abbreviated story goes something like this: Esmé the father came to Scotland from France in 1579, invited by the Scottish Council, possibly to give guidance to the teenaged King James, then thirteen years old. Esmé was himself in his mid-thirties. Despite the age gap, James was completely smitten with this handsome, sophisticated man, an indication of James's yearning for

---

[1] For a consideration of the Folio dedication, see David M. Bergeron, *Textual Patronage in English Drama, 1570–1640* (Aldershot, UK: Ashgate, 2006), 141–57.

affection.[2] The king showered Esmé with titles and gifts, including the title Duke of Lennox. Such a meteoric rise by the Frenchman frightened and challenged the Scottish nobles and the Scottish Kirk. In late 1582, they forced James, then their prisoner, to exile Esmé, who returned to France in late December 1582 and died in May 1583. James managed eventually to escape his captors and sought to assuage his grief by writing a compelling allegorical poem about Esmé called *Phoenix*. In the final l'envoy section, James the poet imagines a new phoenix coming to Scotland, who would be the son Ludovic.

Thus in November 1583, at James's invitation, the nine-year-old Ludovic arrived in Scotland. He would remain a prominent figure at court and a confidant of the king for the rest of his life, never returning to France to live. Honors, titles, and money flowed now to Ludovic, who inherited his father's title as Duke of Lennox. He became Lord Chamberlain of Scotland. And in 1589 when James left Scotland to go to Denmark to marry Anne, the king chose the fifteen-year-old Lennox as presiding officer of the Privy Council—an extraordinary statement about his importance and James's dependence on him. Not surprisingly, when in 1603 James learned of Queen Elizabeth's death and his designation as King of England, he immediately asked Lennox to accompany him to this new land. By this time Lennox's brother, retaining the French title of Lord Aubigny, had arrived in Scotland and also made the transition to the new kingdom. The Stuart brothers became Gentlemen of the Bedchamber, members of the Privy Council, and inductees into the Order of the Garter, among many other offices. (Philip Herbert also became a Gentleman of the Bedchamber, but William, to his chagrin, never did.) Lennox in 1613 became Earl of Richmond and finally Duke of Richmond in 1623, a few months before his death. He was thus the only nobleman to hold both a Scottish and an English ducal title.

In the latest biography of Ben Jonson, Ian Donaldson claims that the Stuart brothers were "keen" theatergoers, a view echoed a few years

---

[2] For a discussion of Esmé and James's relationship, see David M. Bergeron, *King James and Letters of Homoerotic Desire* (Iowa City: University of Iowa Press, 1999).

later by Tom Cain in his edition of *Sejanus*.[3] This statement certainly has plausibility, although neither Donaldson nor Cain offers any concrete evidence. We can place Lennox at theatrical performances at Trinity College, Cambridge University in March 1613, when he accompanied Prince Charles and Prince Frederick, newly married to Princess Elizabeth the previous month. They saw two different plays, both in Latin; one lasted seven to eight hours.[4] This experience would not, however, represent the usual idea of "theatergoing." Cain goes a step further by claiming: "The Stuart brothers are, indeed, the most likely courtiers to have pushed James, who was not himself greatly interested in such matters, to move so quickly to issue the patent for the King's Men" (2:200). This claim—that the Stuart brothers had an instrumental role in bringing the major adult acting companies under royal patronage—is hard to substantiate. The brothers' involvement with the theater, on the other hand, can certainly be documented. I proceed by looking first at Lennox, then Esmé.

While in Scotland, Lennox helped plan and then participated in the royal entry pageant that officially welcomed the king and the new queen to Edinburgh in May 1590. Similarly, in late August 1594, Lennox functioned actively in all the festivities that surrounded the baptism of Prince Henry at Stirling Castle. Thus, we cannot be surprised that he showed similar interests once he came to England; indeed, he helped plan the first Jacobean masque, performed at Hampton Court on New Year's 1604. Evidence for this derives from Dudley Carleton's letter to John Chamberlain. Unfortunately, no text of the masque exists, which some have named the *Masque of the Orient Knights*.[5] Carleton writes of the various festivities at court, including the observation that on the night of New

---

[3] Ian Donaldson, *Ben Jonson: A Life* (Oxford: Oxford Univ. Press, 2011), 186; *Sejanus*, ed. Tom Cain, in *The Cambridge Edition of the Works of Ben Jonson* (Cambridge, UK: Cambridge Univ. Press, 2012), 2:200. In Andrew Gurr's *Playgoing in Shakespeare's London* (Cambridge, UK: Cambridge Univ. Press, 1987), appendix 1, "Playgoers 1567–1642," Gurr does not list either brother.

[4] Information derived from John Hacket, *Scrinia Reserata* (London, 1692), 24.

[5] The suggestion comes from Leeds Barroll in his *Anna of Denmark, Queen of England: A Cultural Biography* (Philadelphia: Univ. of Pennsylvania Press, 2001), 83. Barroll calls Lennox the *rector chori* for the masque, 81.

Year's 1604 the court first saw a "play of Robin Goodfellow and a mask brought in by a magician of China."[6] According to Carleton, Lennox led the all-male corps of eight masquers, who danced and "called out" a comparable group of women, beginning with Anne and those of her inner circle. Esmé and the Herbert brothers also participated. Although Carleton complains that "their attire was rich but somewhat too heavy and cumbersome for dancers" (54), Lennox had made an indelible impression on the new court. On 8 January, Lennox also danced in the masque arranged by Queen Anne and written by Samuel Daniel, *The Vision of the Twelve Goddesses*.

Lennox performed in Jonson's *Hymenaei* on 5 (masque) and 6 (barriers) January 1606, in honor of the marriage of the Earl of Essex and Frances Howard—a marriage apparently not made in heaven. Lennox appeared in the indoor tilt or barriers where he led the sixteen knights who represented champions for Truth, who fought vigorously and successfully against Opinion's supporters until suddenly "light seemed to fill all the hall, and out of it an angel or messenger of glory appearing."[7] Similarly, on 9 February 1608, Lennox, along with his brother and others, danced in Jonson's *The Haddington Masque*, in honor of the marriage of John Ramsey to Elizabeth Radcliffe. Jonson characterizes the masquers' performance as "magnificent and illustrious" (118).

Lennox took active part in the various tournaments that occurred in the early years of James's reign, such as the regular Accession Day tilts (each 24 March). For example, he competed in the one in 1606, although one account complains of lackluster performance and the lack of stunning costumes.[8] That could not be said of the 1610 tournament. This joust at Whitehall included triumphal chariots that conveyed allegorical characters who delivered speeches of compliment to the king. A contemporary account describes the

---

[6] *Dudley Carleton to John Chamberlain 1603–1624: Jacobean Letters*, ed. Maurice Lee, Jr. (New Brunswick, NJ: Rutgers Univ. Press, 1972), 53.

[7] *Ben Jonson: The Complete Masques*, ed. Stephen Orgel (New Haven, CT: Yale Univ. Press, 1969), 104.

[8] See Alan Young, *Tudor and Jacobean Tournaments* (London: George Philip, 1987), 41.

costume: "The Duke of Lennox exceeded all in feathers."[9] (One longs for an illustration of Lennox bedecked in feathers!) He had also been active in Prince Henry's Barriers on 6 January 1610, for which Jonson wrote the speeches. Here Lennox served as one of six who assisted the prince in his martial feats against all comers.

In honor of the visit of King Christian IV of Denmark, brother of Queen Anne, in July–August 1606, Lennox participated in the civic pageant that unfolded in London's streets on 31 July. Lennox had also planned "a challenge to be issued by certain knights of the Fortunate Island" throughout Europe.[10] This ambitious plan got scaled back to England only, but the tilt did take place on 5 August with Lennox and Christian participating. Although it lacked the romantic luster that Lennox had intended, a version of it survives in John Ford's *Honor Triumphant* (1606), which includes the challenges that four knights would have given. In fact, Ford dedicates the first section to "the Right Noble Lord, the Duke of Lennox his Grace."[11] Lennox represents the chivalric argument that "Knights in Ladies service have no free-will." Ford's dedication underscores the slightly over twenty texts that various writers dedicated to Lennox.

George Chapman takes a place in that number. Lennox intervened to help prevent Chapman's arrest for his play *The Conspiracy and Tragedy of Byron*, performed in 1608. The play had stirred the antipathy and anger of the French Ambassador, who convinced Robert Cecil to issue a warrant for Chapman's arrest. A letter survives from Chapman in which he thanks Lennox for the "Shelter" he has been accorded during the "Austeritie of the offended time."[12] Chapman may literally mean "Shelter," as Jonson did in reference to Esmé. In the following year (1609) Chapman offered praise for Lennox in a dedicatory sonnet to his translation of *The Iliad*. A

---

[9] A report from Dudley Carleton, quoted in G. P. V. Akrigg, *Jacobean Pageant, or The Court of King James I* (London: Hamish Hamilton, 1962), 162.

[10] E. K. Chambers, *The Elizabethan Stage* (Oxford: Clarendon Press, 1923), 1:147.

[11] John Ford, *Honor Triumphant* (London, 1606), sig. B1.

[12] Cited by Richard Dutton, *Mastering the Revels: The Regulation and Censorship of English Renaissance Drama* (Iowa City: Univ. of Iowa Press, 1991), 185.

series of such sonnets follows book 12, but one directed to Lennox occupies the first place. The heading is: "To the right Gracious and worthy, the Duke of LENNOX, &c."[13] Chapman begins: "Amongst th' Heroes of the Worlds prime years, / Stand here, great Duke, and see them shine about you." The poet concludes: "To this soule, then, your gracious count'nance give; / That gave, to such as you, such meanes to live." Like the heroes of the past, Lennox will "live ever."

As we know, King James brought London's adult acting companies under royal patronage in May 1603, shortly after his arrival in England. Nevertheless, other companies continued to exist under the patronage of noblemen, including the Duke of Lennox. About his troupe we know relatively little. No records exist of performances by them in London; instead, they seem to have been a traveling company of actors. An early record of the Duke of Lennox's Men can be found in the Dulwich Manuscripts that relate to Henslowe's *Diary*, an entry dating from 13 October 1604. In this warrant, Lennox addresses mayors, justices of the peace, and others "on behalf of his company of players, who had apparently been forbidden to act."[14] Another item in this collection "is a bond from Francis Henslowe to Philip Henslowe in £60 to observe certain articles of agreement between Francis, John Garland and Abraham Saverie, 'his ffelowes, servantes to the most noble Prince the duke of Lennox,' dated 16 March 1605." From this we learn at least some of the actors' names. As Chambers notes, both Garland and Henslowe had been Queen Elizabeth's men, and "it is possible that when these men were left stranded by her death in 1603, they found a new patron in Lennox."[15]

Thanks to the *Records of Early English Drama*, we discover some of the places where the Duke of Lennox's Men performed: Canterbury (two weeks in April 1604), earning 13.s 4d.; Norwich Common Hall (8 April 1604); Barnstaple, Devon, Guildhall (September

---

[13] Chapman, *Homer Prince of Poets* (London, 1609), following 118. The editors and printer of the Shakespeare Folio adopt this same practice of an "&c" following the nobleman's name.

[14] *Henslowe's Diary*, 2nd edition, ed. R. A. Foakes (Cambridge, UK: Cambridge Univ. Press, 2002), 298.

[15] Chambers, *Elizabethan Stage*, 2:241. Chambers derives much of his information from John Tucker Murray, *English Dramatic Companies 1558–1642* (London: Constable, 1910), 1:228–29.

1604–September 1605); St Mary's Guildhall, Coventry (November 1604–October 1605); St Mary's Coventry again (November 1607–October 1608); Bath, Somerset, Guildhall (May 1609–September 1609). A final entry appears for a performance in Folkestone, Kent, Town Hall (September 1617–September 1618), earning 1s.[16] Lennox also had a company of trumpeters, who may have on occasion accompanied the players. These entries tantalize us because so much remains unrecorded and therefore unknown. The last one in Folkestone is puzzling because it comes so late and with payment of a measly one shilling. We learn nothing about what this company may have performed—kinds of plays, let alone titles of plays. For at least ten years and possibly longer, however, these players owed their protection and support to Lennox.

Some scholars have claimed that Lennox also arranged for a performance of *Pericles* on 20 May 1619 at Whitehall. G. E. Bentley reports in *Jacobean and Caroline Stage*: "The Duke of Lennox had *Pericles* performed in the King's Great Chamber after supper for the departing French Ambassador."[17] John Astington in an appendix to his book on court theater lists the Duke of Lennox as "sponsor" for the *Pericles* court performance.[18] More recently, Katherine Duncan-Jones in her 2010 Shakespeare biography confirms this information: "The Duke of Lennox arranged for it [*Pericles*] to be performed for a French delegation at Whitehall Palace on 20 May 1619."[19] Bentley depended on E. K. Chambers's *William Shakespeare*;[20] Chambers had himself relied on an apparent transcription of a letter from Gerrard

---

[16] This information comes from a distillation of *REED* materials found on their "Patrons and Performances" Web page, accessed May 29, 2016, https://reed.library.utoronto.ca/. For more information consult *Coventry*, ed. R. W. Ingram (Manchester: Manchester Univ. Press, 1981); *Norwich 1540–1642*, ed. David Galloway (Toronto: Univ. of Toronto Press, 1984); and *Devon*, ed. John M. Wasson (Toronto: Univ. of Toronto Press, 1986).

[17] G. E. Bentley, *Jacobean and Caroline Stage* (Oxford: Oxford Univ. Press, 1968), 7:31.

[18] John H. Astington, *English Court Theatre 1558–1642* (Cambridge, UK: Cambridge Univ. Press, 1999), 252.

[19] Katherine Duncan-Jones, *Shakespeare: An Ungentle Life* (London: Methuen, 2010), 237.

[20] E. K. Chambers, *William Shakespeare: A Study of Facts and Problems* (Oxford: Clarendon Press, 1930).

Herbert to Dudley Carleton, published by J. O. Halliwell in 1865.[21] Likewise, F. D. Hoeninger (1962) and Suzanne Gossett (2004), editors of the Arden *Pericles*, also rely on Halliwell. Yet Halliwell does not indicate the source for the Herbert letter. Duncan-Jones cites Egerton MS 2592 in the British Library, but it does not specify *Pericles* as the play performed, nor does it give credit to Lennox for planning it. I have examined the original document, which resides in the State Papers in the National Archives, London, and can verify that Lennox did host the elaborate feast that took place, but the text does not say that Lennox arranged for the *Pericles* production. My study of this letter raises doubts about Lennox's *sponsoring* a performance of *Pericles* at court in 1619, no matter how much I want to believe it.

Now I turn to Esmé Stuart, who also served as patron of a minor acting company, Lord Aubigny's players, for which *REED* turns up only two records of performance: Congleton, Cheshire (1613), and St Mary's Guildhall, Coventry (1613–14). Esmé certainly had a serious involvement with playwrights and the theater. We know, for example, that he supported Ben Jonson in many ways, including having Jonson live in his house for a period of at least five years, probably beginning in 1604, during one of Jonson's several disputes with his wife.[22] Both men lived in Blackfriars, making frequent contact likely. Clearly

---

[21] J. O. Halliwell, *A Copy of a Letter of News Written to Sir Dudley Carleton, at the Hague, in May, 1619* (London, 1865). Halliwell does not indicate the source for this letter. At the end of this privately printed book, Halliwell penned this curious note, found in the British Library copy: "Fifteen copies destroyed by me 5 April, 1865. Ten only preserved. Number Ten." According to Marvin Spevack, Halliwell often destroyed copies, apparently hoping to drive up their value. See Marvin Spevack, *James Orchard Halliwell-Phillipps* (New Castle, DE: Oak Knoll Press, 2001), 257. The *Calendar of State Papers Domestic, 1619–1623* (London, 1858), 47, #46, indicates a performance of *Pericles* at the banquet on 20 May 1619. The original document can be found in SP 14/109, fols. 100–101 in the National Archives, London.

[22] There has been a fair amount of dispute and uncertainty about exactly when Jonson lived in the Stuart house. Ian Donaldson examines the theories, ranging from two different times of residency to a much later date, in his *Ben Jonson*, 470–71n21. Donaldson opts for one period beginning probably in 1604. It is surprising that the latest biographical entry about Esmé, the article in the *Oxford Dictionary of National Biography*, makes no mention of this patron's connection to Jonson.

Jonson enjoyed numerous benefits from his close association with Esmé, among which would have been remarkable access to powerful noblemen. In all likelihood, Esmé supported Jonson with an annual pension, as did others, including, eventually, King James himself.

The year 1605 presented several challenges for Jonson—challenges that Esmé helped him confront. Jonson had already had difficulties with his play *Sejanus*, beyond the initial dismal audience reaction to its performance in 1603 or 1604. He had been summoned to appear before the Privy Council and defend himself and the content of his play. This led to some self-censorship by the time of the play's publication in 1605. A few of Jonson's acquaintances had been involved in the Gunpowder Plot, which raised further suspicions about him. That year also brought a performance and publication of *Eastward Ho!* on which Jonson had collaborated with Chapman and John Marston. Because of presumed offenses to the Scots in the play, the three playwrights ended up in prison, a punishment that seems out of all proportion to the alleged "crimes" in this delightful comedy. The play received a performance in 1613 that occasioned no stir. Possibly the 1605 quarto had been modified before publication, thus making it difficult for us to see what all the fuss was about.

We do know that Chapman and Jonson busily wrote letters that sought help in gaining release from prison. A discovery in the early part of the twentieth century provides the evidence for the letters, seven from Jonson and three from Chapman, all addressed to obvious people, such as the king, the Lord Chamberlain, Robert Cecil, Philip Herbert, and Esmé Stuart. In a letter to Thomas Howard, Earl of Suffolk and Lord Chamberlain, Chapman thanks Suffolk for his aid and attributes Jonson's pardon to the intervention of Esmé. Chapman writes: "we are with all humility enforced to solicit the propagation of your most noble favours to our present freedom: and the rather since we hear from Lord D'Awbney, that his Highness hath remitted one of us wholly to your Lordship's favour. And that the other had still your Lordship's passing noble remembrance for his joint liberty."[23] Jonson wrote Esmé, possibly after his release: "The noble favours you have done us, most worthy Lord, cannot be so concealed or removed but that they have broke in upon us even where we lie double bound

---

[23] Quoted in the New Mermaids edition of *Eastward Ho!* ed. C. G. Petter (London: Ernest Benn, 1973), 127.

to their comforts" (131). Jonson discounts the possibility that this lord has done any of this for his own personal ambition, and adds: "yet be pleased to take this protestation, that, next his Majesty's favour, I shall not covet that thing more in the world than to express the lasting gratitude I have conceived in soul towards your Lordship." Esmé's intervention gives a fuller meaning to the idea of patronage beyond mere support for publication.

In the 1616 Folio, Jonson included *Epigrams*; in number 127, he commends Esmé. In all likelihood, Jonson wrote the poem much earlier, perhaps even in 1605 when the two men had an intense connection. Whenever Jonson wrote it, he repays the patronage that Esmé had extended to him. Jonson begins: "Is there a hope that man would thankful be / If I should fail in gratitude to thee, / To whom I am so bound, loved Aubigny? / No."[24] Jonson calls for all posterity to note his indebtedness: "How full of want, how swallowed up, how dead / I and this muse had been if thou hadst not / Lent timely succours, and new life beget." What an extraordinary claim: Esmé had provided Jonson with new life, comprising artistic life and physical nurture. In many ways, Jonson suggests, he can never repay the benefits and patronage that he has received from Aubigny: influence that helped release him from prison, financial support, housing, and artistic resurrection.

We cannot therefore be surprised also to find in the Jonson Folio the dedication of *Sejanus* to Esmé.[25] Jonson omits from the Folio all addresses to readers found in the earlier quarto texts, replacing them with dedications to noblemen. As I have observed elsewhere, this "decision reinforces the Folio as a monumental text that desires to place itself in the aura of aristocratic patronage."[26] This situation leads me to a paradox: "in this most self-conscious readerly text, Jonson deflects his connections with readers, opting instead to honor aristocrats and friends."

---

[24] *Ben Jonson*, ed. Ian Donaldson (Oxford: Oxford Univ. Press, 1985), 273.

[25] For some odd reason Donaldson in the Jonson biography first says that the 1605 quarto edition of *Sejanus* contains the dedication to Aubigny (182); but then correctly says on page 186 that it was the Folio edition that has such a dedication.

[26] *Textual Patronage in English Drama*, 131.

The brief dedication to Esmé reads as follows from the Folio:

> If ever any ruine were so great, as to survive; I thinke this be one that I send you: the Fal of Sejanus. It is a poeme, that (if I well remember) in your Lordship's sight suffer'd no lesse violence from our people here, then the subject of it did from the rage of the people of Rome; but, with a different fate, as (I hope) merit: For this hath out-liv'd their malice, and begot itselfe a greater favour then he lost, the love of good men. Amongst whom, if I make your Lordship the first it thankes, it is not without a just confession of the bond your benefits have, and ever shall hold upon me.[27]

Clearly, the failure and dispute over *Sejanus*, some dozen years earlier, still rankles in Jonson's memory and soul. And yet the play survives, having outlived the "malice" that others had displayed toward it. Jonson implies that Esmé Stuart may have been among the early audiences.

Publishing *Sejanus* again in the 1616 collection underscores Jonson's devotion to the play. It also offers him a chance, given the apparent agenda of the Folio, to single out Esmé Stuart's support of him, the "love of good men" that Jonson refers to. Indeed, Stuart stands as the "first" deserving thanks, which only reinforces the "bond your benefits have, and ever shall hold upon me." This epistle dedicatory and *Epigram 127* complement and expand each other, providing an unmistakable picture of Jonson's gratitude for Esmé's patronage. This prefatory document in the text of *Sejanus* illustrates how a playwright, and this one in particular, could seize the opportunity "to stake out his own view. For Jonson this becomes an essential part of the construction of authorship, one skillfully navigating among the shoals of political power in a textual economy of patronage."[28]

Even if we cannot be precise about the Stuart brothers' habits of theater attendance, we can certainly see from this sketchy survey that the theater world came to them, seeking their intervention, support, housing, and patronage. Surely they deserve some place in

---

[27] Ben Jonson, *The Workes of Benjamin Jonson* (London, 1616), 357. I have slightly modernized some spelling.

[28] Bergeron, *Textual Patronage*, 134.

the pantheon of Jacobean theater enthusiasts. The Herbert brothers might need to share some space in our adulation with the equally compelling Stuart brothers.

The University of Kansas

"You would pluck out the heart of my mystery": The Audience in *Hamlet*

John N. Wall

W HEN we think about Shakespeare's plays, we tend to think of them as closed worlds, each one a system of actions and interactions among characters involved in plots that begin, develop, and work their way to their conclusions. So our discussions about what happens in these plays are framed in terms that place the issues of the play and the sources of information needed to resolve those issues within the play itself, or in its originating culture—as phenomena "over there" in the world of the play, very much apart from us, who are "over here," in our own worlds. This style of consideration is of course exacerbated in conversations among literary scholars because for us Shakespeare's plays are texts that appear to us as black marks on the white pages of scholarly editions.

Recent trends in theatrical performance, however, raise questions about whether this separation between the play—"over there" in its own world—and us—the play's readers or observers, in the case of actual performances—might be an artificial one. I'm thinking of the increasing interest among theater professionals in recovering original styles of performance practices for productions of early modern plays. At London's Globe Theater reconstruction, for example, or at the American Shakespeare Center in Staunton, Virginia, the "house style" of performance deliberately seeks to recreate—and to incorporate into their productions—the conditions of performance in early modern theatres. For productions at the Blackfriars Theatre in Staunton, for example, they "Do It With the Lights On," while at the Wanamaker Theatre in London performances take place not just in uniform illumination but in a space lit only by candlelight. Less frequent, but in the same spirit of incorporating original theatrical and cultural practices, is the occasional practice of performing early modern drama in "Original Pronunciation," using the hypothetical reconstruction of early modern London pronunciation devised by the linguist David Crystal.

One characteristic of productions done in the spirit of adopting "original practices" in contemporary performance has been to incorporate into stage productions an aggressive effort to efface the fourth wall that separates the world of the play in performance and the audience assembled to watch it. In such productions, there comes to be a real sense in which the audience ceases to be passive observers of the unfolding action of the play "over there" and, at least in a limited way, become performers in the play itself, as the "play world" of the stage or performance space extends to encompass the interior of the theatre and incorporate into itself the previously separated world of the audience.

So, in this style of production, if we in the audience have become actors in the play, how do we learn our parts? Actors at the Globe and at the American Shakespeare Center help by seeking, in the moment-by-moment unfolding of the action, opportunities for engaging directly with us. Soliloquies are staged as conversations with the audience; at Staunton, audience members are invited to sit on stage and are involved directly in the unfolding action by, for example, holding props for the actors. At the Globe in London, performers arrive on stage by making their way through the audience; this can be especially entertaining when actors have to push through the crowd of groundlings standing in the pit and blocking their way. Again at the Globe, the thrust stage of traditional design is frequently augmented by further extension into the audience's space, making it possible in a recent production of *Much Ado about Nothing* for the actor playing Beatrice—when she realizes that not only does Benedict love her, but that she loves Benedict—to kneel down on the stage and joyfully embrace a member of the audience.

My argument in this essay is that—at least in the case of *Hamlet*, that most metatheatrical of plays—the play itself is intended to engage us in ways that draw us into active participation in the action of the play. Jerry Mills once said of *Hamlet*, in my presence, that we might profit, when thinking of *Hamlet*, if we regarded it as a mystery story. By this, he did not mean simply that many things about *Hamlet* are abiding mysteries, resistant to our "plucking out" their hearts, but that we might profit from regarding it as an example of the mystery genre, a detective story, in which the focus of the action involves characters seeking, or concealing, or revealing truths behind mysteries.

After all, as we well know, *Hamlet* begins with a question— "Who's there?"—and most of the characters in the play spend a great deal of their time trying to make sense of partial information, trying out theories of why people behave in certain ways and testing these theories against information gained from the Ghost, from spying (as Claudius and Polonius do to observe one of Hamlet's encounters with Ophelia), from asking others to observe someone's behavior (as Claudius and Gertrude request of Rosencrantz and Guildenstern), or from setting up situations for characters and observing their responses to them (as Hamlet does with Claudius in his staging of *The Murder of Gonzago*).

In a very real sense, therefore, the behavior of many of the characters in this most enigmatic and mysterious of plays may well be characterized by saying that they are all playing detective. So my argument is that, like the characters onstage in this play, we too are given the challenge of unraveling unclear sequences of events, unknown motives, mysterious behaviors, and secret messages. Thus in *Hamlet*, as in more familiar examples of the mystery story genre, we find ourselves provided by the play with a very specific role, one that parallels those played by the actors on stage: the role of trying to understand—given limited and often perplexing information— what is going on, who knows what, and when they know it.

A mystery story is, after all, a genre of fiction that is especially about structuring the experience of the audience. In a mystery story the play of knowledge and ignorance, the questioning of motive and meaning, and the opportunity to discern fact in the midst of confusing alternatives are structured for the reader as well as for the characters in the story. The experience of a mystery story is not simply one of passively following along with the detective in the gathering and sifting of facts, the testing of suspects' stories, the search for which of the suspects had motive, means, and opportunity. Inevitably we become engaged in the process of detection itself, trying to unravel the mystery of whodunit before the detective does. The mystery story invites us, through the gradual unfolding of clues, to anticipate the outcome, to solve the puzzle of the crime. Of course, because the mystery writer is staging the flow of information—and misdirection—for us, we inevitably discover that the mystery writer holds all the cards, that the detective is always ahead of us, so that the ending always comes as a surprise for us.

So, my claim in this essay is not only that *Hamlet* is a kind of mystery story, but also that in this play we in the audience are not allowed to play the passive role of observer, but instead are called upon and provided with the resources to play an active role, a role created for us by the way that information of various kinds is disclosed or withheld throughout the course of the action. I want to use this insight—that the mystery story casts a role for its audience as coinvestigators in the resolution of the mystery—to make three points about *Hamlet*. One is that the flow of information we are given as the plot of the play unfolds often puts us in possession of specific knowledge that enables us to understand events in ways that ally us with some characters and not with others. We know, for example, from the opening scene of the play that Horatio, Barnado, and Marcellus plan to tell Hamlet about their sighting of the ghost of Hamlet Sr. As a result, when they come on stage in act 1, scene 2, where Hamlet is finishing up the "too, too sullied flesh" soliloquy, we know what they are going to tell Hamlet. But Hamlet doesn't.

Second, as characters on stage are observing what strikes them as strange or unusual behavior, and are trying to figure out what that behavior means or what causes it, the audience, too, is given enough information to join in that speculation. In the case of *Hamlet*, while the characters on stage wonder about what is happening and why, we in the audience are given a shifting array of information; sometimes we know things before Hamlet does, and sometimes Hamlet knows things before we do. Sometimes we watch Hamlet learn things that we already know; sometimes Hamlet acts on the basis of information we already have, but sometimes he acts on the basis of information we don't have. Sometimes we believe we know things that explain actions taken on stage; in these situations, events unfold in ways that reaffirm our understanding of what is happening. Other times we think we know things that explain what is happening on stage, but in the process of these events unfolding before us, we have reason to question our understanding.

Third, not only the ebb and flow of information but also the unfolding of the plot in a mystery story has implications for our experience of *Hamlet*. While the basic plot of a mystery story is about the discovery of truth and the revealing of mystery, it is also about the restoration of order to a world where order has been disturbed by the crime that initiates the plot. In these terms, the death of Hamlet, Sr. is not only an act of fratricide but also a disruption of the ordinary course of events in Denmark. Without Hamlet Sr.'s death, he would have lived out his life with Gertrude as his queen, presumably to be succeeded by his son. Claudius would have lived out his life, presumably envious of his brother's power and consumed by unrequited desire for his sister-in-law. Fortinbras would not have had an opportunity, without the disruption of order, to raise an army to invade Denmark, or whatever country happened to be both accessible and vulnerable.

In this counterfactual version of *Hamlet*, neither Laertes nor Hamlet would have come home from college in the middle of their semesters. Neither Horatio, Rosencrantz, nor Guildenstern, not to mention the Players, would have come to Elsinore. Hamlet might have married Ophelia, or he might not have, since, as Laertes rightly says, in matters of matrimony, Hamlet's "will is not his own." Finally, in this alternative universe, there would be no need for the sequence of events that leads to the Ghost of Hamlet Sr.'s disturbance of the night, Claudius's public disclosure of his crime, Polonius's death, Hamlet's painful bedtime conversation with his mother, nor his murder-by-proxy of Rosencrantz and Guildenstern, Ophelia's death, or the staged murder of Hamlet by Laertes and Claudius.

By the end of *Hamlet,* however, all these events are headed toward a renewed sense of the predictable. Even though at the end of the play we have been through an orgy of fighting, confession, poisoning, and death worthy of *A Game of Thrones*, at the end Claudius is dead and Hamlet and Laertes are reconciled. Hamlet is able to see ahead clearly enough to predict that Fortinbras will take over the throne of Denmark, and to bless that future. And so it comes to be. Truth is revealed in this scene—in the case of who killed Hamlet Sr., surely, but also in the case of how life in Denmark will go on.

With that sketch of my argument, therefore, let us go back to the beginning, to our basic point that the audience in *Hamlet* is a character in its own right, an active rather than passive participant in the progress of the play's interactions. The shifting communication of information—sometimes we are "in the know," but sometimes we aren't, sometimes we think we are in the know, but we turn out not to be—all this invites us to be actively engaged as observers, sharing the inquisitive behavior, the testing strategies, and the persistent efforts to get the answer right that obsess so many of *Hamlet*'s characters.

We know, for example, a possible explanation for Hamlet's strange behavior when Ophelia first reports it to her father in act 2, scene 1:

> as I was sewing in my closet,
> Lord Hamlet, with his doublet all unbraced,
> No hat upon his head, his stockings fouled,
> Ungartered, and down-gyvèd to his ankle,
> Pale as his shirt, his knees knocking each other,
> And with a look so piteous in purport
> As if he had been loosèd out of hell
> To speak of horrors—he comes before me

We know this explanation, of course, because we have heard—only a short time before Ophelia's account of her experience—Hamlet warn Horatio, Barnado, and Marcellus that he may "put an antic disposition on." So while Ophelia is frightened and amazed at Hamlet's behavior and Polonius is smugly confident that this is an expression of Hamlet's melancholy over his unrequited love for Ophelia, we sit there smugly confident in our own right that we, as part of the audience for Hamlet's confidential description of his plans to cope with life in Elsinore after the ghost's revelations, at least think we know what he's up to.

We may well, of course, have second thoughts about what Hamlet is doing in this scene. Those who believe that Hamlet is deranged in his behavior here of course reject the idea that his behavior is calculated. And I have often wondered why Hamlet—if he is trying out his "antic behavior" performance in this scene—tries it out first on Ophelia, who, other than Horatio, might well be Hamlet's only friend in Denmark. Why Hamlet would set out to alienate her as the first performance of his "antic disposition" *persona* is, therefore, not at all clear. One might well imagine Hamlet taking her into his confidence, encouraging her to feel sympathy for the predicament he is in after the Ghost has insisted that he take up the plot of revenge tragedy. Yet there he is, "with his doublet all unbraced, / No hat upon his head, his stockings fouled, / Ungartered, and down-gyvèd to his ankle, / Pale as his shirt, his knees knocking each other."

My point here is not that the special bits of knowledge we gain because we are present with the characters when special information is disclosed necessarily determine our interpretation of the action or of people's behavior. That is to say, special information shapes, or guides, or at least suggests possible avenues for the interpretive journey we—along with the characters onstage—are on in this play. Our possession of the information—or even our having questions about the accuracy of the information—calls us to experience the same sorts of relief the play's characters have when they believe that the unfolding of events affirms their understanding of what is happening—as well as the same experience of uncertainty the characters also have when events do not go as their understanding prepares them to believe they will. Thus the ebb and flow of information we share with the characters on stage puts us into the process of the play's unfolding, or perhaps more precisely, into the predicament that so many of the characters in this play share with each other, regardless of what side or what interpretive position they come to hold. They engage in speculation, testing, and plotting; they teach us how to play the part we in the audience are given.

This ebb and flow of confidence and uncertainty shifts as our awareness and possession of special knowledge comes and goes. I have already commented on our advance knowledge of the content of the message that Horatio, Barnardo, and Marcellus will deliver to Hamlet when they approach him in act 1, scene 2, knowledge that we have gained through spending time with these characters on the parapet of Elsinore Castle, observing their interaction with the ghost, their recognition that he looks like King Hamlet, and their determination to share all this information with Hamlet himself. They say they will convey this information to Hamlet, and we watch them do so.

Other occasions when we know things that Hamlet remains ignorant of include: the occasion when Claudius and Polonius plot to spy on Hamlet and then carry out their plot while Hamlet talks with Ophelia; Claudius and Gertrude's plotting with Rosencrantz and Guildenstern for them to spy on Hamlet, which they do, and report back to the King and Queen; Polonius's decision to hide behind the arras in Gertrude's bedroom while she talks with Hamlet. On these occasions, when Hamlet is being spied upon, as we know it, we in effect join in the perspective of the spies, or have a kind of double consciousness, sharing Hamlet's experience of the scene vicariously, while we share the perspective of the play's spies, watching Hamlet's behavior from our seats as they watch his behavior from behind whatever convenient hiding place they can find.

We know also—from Polonius's conversation with his daughter on the occasion of Laertes's leave-taking for France—that he is very concerned about his daughter Ophelia's relationship with Hamlet; thus we are not surprised when she rushes to him after her encounter with Hamlet in her closet. We know, from hearing Claudius and Gertrude ask Rosencrantz and Guildenstern to spy on Hamlet, that they are working for the King and Queen, so it comes as no surprise when Hamlet is quickly able to unmask the real reason they are at Elsinore.

When Hamlet asks Ophelia "Where's your father?" in act 3, scene 1, line 141, many directors choose to let this be a sign that Hamlet knows he is being spied on, at least by Polonius. As a result, they interject into the play some event, some sound or movement on the part of Polonius or Claudius that allows Hamlet to become aware of their presence. This may be because they are building on Hamlet's previously displayed prowess as a detective from act 2, scene 2, when Hamlet so quickly penetrates Rosencrantz and Guildenstern's disguise as his friends, challenging them to tell "me whether you were sent for or no." On the other hand, if one wants Hamlet to know he is being spied on in act 3, that disclosure can come at any time and if it comes early enough in the scene, suddenly Hamlet's "To be or not to be" soliloquy ceases to be a soliloquy but a performance delivered with Claudius and Polonius joining us in the audience.

We also know, both from Hamlet's discussion with the actors about their performance of the *Murder of Gonzago* and from his "rogue and peasant slave" soliloquy, in which he tells us that "the play's the thing wherein I'll catch the conscience of the king," that the actors' performance is a trap to provoke Claudius into disclosing incriminating information. We know also that Hamlet is concerned more about his mother's hasty remarriage than he is about Claudius becoming king instead of Hamlet, so we are not really surprised that he accuses Gertrude of inappropriate behavior when they are together in her bedchamber. We also, of course, know from Claudius's conversations with Laertes that Hamlet, at the end of the play, is walking into a trap, that the odds are against him, that death threatens him from several different directions.

There are moments in the play, however, when our knowledge comes in bits and pieces, with a resulting evolution in our experience of the play. In act 3, scene 3, Claudius, immediately after being tricked by Hamlet into a revealing response to the *Murder of Gonzago*, laments his crime, wonders if he can be forgiven since he still has the fruits of his treachery—his throne and his queen—and kneels to pray. Hamlet comes in, sees him, decides to kill the king, then equivocates because he fears Claudius might find forgiveness from God, and leaves with the act of revenge undone. We are still there after he leaves; then Claudius rises to claim he has found no peace, and we—and we alone—recognize that Claudius's life was in danger, and that had Hamlet killed the king at that opportune moment he would have achieved his revenge.

Sometimes we find that we have acquired information that helps us distance ourselves from the characters onstage as they form their own opinions. At the end of act 3, scene 1, Polonius is still arguing for his claim that Hamlet is infected with love melancholy. We may have considered his argument seriously earlier in the play, but now we know far too much to do so. Sometimes we discover we need information we do not have. I never cease to be puzzled that Hamlet can go from lecturing Ophelia about her sex life and ordering her: "get thee to a nunnery," in act 3, scene 1, to asking her if he can "lie in her lap" just a few minutes of stage time and a hundred lines of text later

There are moments in *Hamlet* as well in which we realize that the information we have been given is designed to confuse rather than to clarify, that the spirit presiding over the structure of the play has had his way with us, has deliberately—for purposes of dramatic development and effect—mislead us. The most glaring example of this happens at the beginning of act 5, scene 1, when Hamlet, having returned from his aborted trip to England, meets his friend Horatio in a graveyard. We first meet a couple of grave-diggers, whose conversation makes clear to us that they are digging the grave of Ophelia. We have heard of Ophelia's death by drowning in the previous act, delivered in a way that has a powerful effect on Laertes, come back to challenge Claudius for the crown. The news of his sister's death disarms him, rendering him vulnerable to Claudius's scheming. Now we are reminded by the gravediggers that her death is irregular, a kind of suicide, which should bar her from burial in hallowed ground, except that the clergy have met and decided that she may be buried—albeit without all the ceremonies of a Requiem Mass.

Enter Hamlet and Horatio, who wind up engaging in a conversation with the gravediggers about the length of time a body will last in the earth, and about whose bones are being dug up to make room for another body. Then the funeral procession approaches. Hamlet notices members of the funeral procession—"Here comes the King, / The Queen, the courtiers." And then wonders, "Who is this they follow?" We know; the gravediggers know; the royal party knows, but Hamlet doesn't. If you were Horatio, having just reunited with Hamlet after his return from sea, don't you think you would have said, "Oh, Hamlet, by the way, I'm sure you will want to know that while you were away your old girlfriend Ophelia died. She killed herself." But he doesn't. Hamlet says, startled, "What, the fair Ophelia?" Hamlet does not know. But, if Hamlet does not know, it is because Horatio hasn't told him. And if Horatio hasn't told him, what are they doing in a graveyard in the first place? Why on earth, given all the other places they might have met for their serious conversation about what happened to Hamlet while he was on his sea voyage, why do they wind up in a graveyard, especially *this* graveyard? And just in time for this funeral?

This is the point in the play at which some force—which Hamlet will later name "Providence"—seems to take over. One way of accounting for the graveyard scene is that Shakespeare wanted this to be about the dramatic and almost violent confrontation between Hamlet and Laertes literally inside Ophelia's grave. That confrontation sets up the complex scene of the game of dueling between Hamlet and Laertes that will end the play. To have that confrontational scene take place, Shakespeare needs all the major players present, in the graveyard, including Hamlet. But to give that scene the dramatic and confrontational quality Shakespeare wanted for it, he needs Hamlet to discover that the body is Ophelia's, the funeral is Ophelia's, suddenly, well into the scene, and not before. But to make that work, Shakespeare needs for us not to think about the fact that there is no reason for Hamlet to be in the graveyard, as though he were coming to Ophelia's funeral, even though he is not.

And it works. Before I started thinking about who knows what and when in this play, and started tracking the flow of information, I certainly never thought much at all about the fact that Hamlet has absolutely no reason to be in that graveyard, and at such a timely moment. It is a commonplace of *Hamlet* criticism at least since the time of Douglas Bush to note that when Hamlet returns from his aborted trip to England, he changes his tone and style of address. Except for Hamlet's comments in response to the unearthing of Yorick's skull, for example, there are no more soliloquies. We know that Claudius and Laertes are plotting against him, and we know that Hamlet—after his uncovering of Claudius's plot to have Hamlet murdered by the King of England—has every reason to be suspicious of Claudius's motives. Yet when Horatio says he believes Hamlet will lose the duel, Hamlet dismisses his concerns on the grounds that he has been training since coming from Wittenberg. When Horatio pushes the point, Hamlet resorts to biblical echo— "there is providence in the fall of a sparrow"—and, in that context, claims that being ready is all one can do.

And so we watch, now, for the first time in the play, passively, as events unfold before us, pretty much as we might expect, given what we know. But Hamlet turns out to be ready. Seizing the moment as it unfolds, Hamlet exposes Claudius's treachery, is reconciled with Laertes, instructs Horatio as to his future role in the course of events, and foretells the future for Denmark's governance. Not a bad seizing of the opportunity that Claudius inadvertently provides for him.

As in the classic mystery story, *Hamlet* opens with an inexplicable death that both serves as the provoking event, providing the subject for the remainder of the plot, and at the same time represents the kind of event that disturbs the settled order of things. It is an interruption in the ordinary—and orderly—ebb and flow of events. We know the play is over when the mystery of the whodunit is solved, but also when order is restored. Shakespeare in *Hamlet* gives us a role to play in the unfolding of events—gives all of us, no matter what our dramatic training, the chance to play a role in *Hamlet*, to join with Hamlet, Claudius, Gertrude, Polonius, Ophelia, and Laertes, in the process of discovery, testing, and plotting that leads us to revelation and resolution. Somewhere in the way Shakespeare shapes our role and gives us the chance to become part of his "traffic of the stage" lies a clue to the abiding mystery of *Hamlet*'s appeal.

North Carolina State University

Spenser's Reformation Epic: Gloriana and the Unadulterated Arthur

Robert Lanier Reid

ANY English poets yearned to write an Arthuriad, presumably to surpass Virgil's canonical *Aeneid* with legends of the English king whose knights took an oath on each Pentecost to be loyal and merciful, to avoid murder and greed, to respect and defend gentlewomen:

> the kynge stablisshed all the knyghtes and gaff hem rychesse and londys; and charged them never to do outerage nothir morthir, and allwayes to fle treson, and to gyff mercy unto hym that askith mercy, upon payne of forfeiture [of their] worship and lordship of kynge Arthure for evermore; and allwayes to do ladyes, damesels, and jantilwomen and wydowes [socour:] strengthe hem in hir ryghtes, and never to enforce them upon payne of dethe. Also that no man take no batayles in a wrongfull quarell for no love ne for no worldis goodis. So unto thys were all knyghtis sworne of the Table Rounde both olde and yonge. And every yere so were the[y] sworne at the high feste of Pentecoste.[1]

In "The Myth of Arthur," the Welsh poet David Jones traces the "native . . . 'English' tradition" idealizing Arthur's rule: "Geoffrey—Wace—Layamon, echoes of Chaucer, Malory of course, Drayton, Camden, Spenser, and almost Milton, who drew back from writing

---

[1] Eugene Vinaver, ed., *The Works of Sir Thomas Malory*, 3rd ed., rev. P. J. C. Field. Oxford: Clarendon Press, 1990, 1330, lines 119–20; Vinaver's emendations.

his Arthuriad and chose the theme of the Fall."[2] Jones writes that Ben Jonson spoke of his "intention to perfect an epic poem entitled *Herologia*, of the worthies of his country, roused by fame, and was to dedicate it to his country. . . . For a heroic poem, he said, there was no such grounds as King Arthur's fiction," and he noted Sidney's intention to transform "all of his *Arcadia* to the stories of King Arthur."[3]

Only Spenser came close to fulfilling this dream. In his "Letter to Ralegh" he calls Arthur "the image of a braue knight, perfected in the twelue priuate morall vertues," his magnificence "the perfection of all the rest, and conteineth in it them all."[4] Is Spenser's hero morally perfect? Does he match the spiritual *Arthurian Torso* that so fired the fantasy of Charles Williams and C. S. Lewis?[5] In the first two legends of *The Faerie Queene* Arthur does overcome two great complementary flaws of human nature: Orgoglio in book 1 is the flesh's assertive pride, shown in apocalyptic context; in book 2 Maleger is the inverse, the flesh's mortal vacuity, shown in a temporal setting. But in both battles Arthur has problems. His potent arms, made by Spenser's Merlin to reflect truths of God and the soul, show Arthur's dependence on both divine and human aid. Like the Redcrosse Knight, Arthur does not understand his weapons, does not know himself, uneasily seeks his origin and destiny. Nor does he attain *progressive* perfection in books 1–6, except by growing frustration as his moral efficacy steadily (and schematically) declines. His hermeneutic bafflement is shared by readers, who puzzle over the strange romance

[2] Jones, "The Myth of Arthur" in *Epoch and Artist*, ed. Harmon Grisewood (London: Faber & Faber, 1959), 214. Cited in David A. Summers, *Spenser's Arthur: The British Arthurian Tradition and The Faerie Queene* (Lanham, MD: Univ. Press of America, 1997), 204.

[3] *Ben Jonson: The Complete Poems*, ed. George Parfitt (New Haven: Yale Univ. Press, 1975), 461, 464.

[4] Edmund Spenser, *The Faerie Queene*, 2nd edition, ed. A. C. Hamilton et al. (Harlow, UK: Pearson, 2007), 715–16. Hereafter cited parenthetically by book, canto, and stanza.

[5] *Arthurian Torso containing the . . . fragment of The Figure of Arthur by Charles Williams and a Commentary on the Arthurian Poems of Charles Williams by C. S. Lewis* (Oxford: Oxford Univ. Press, 1948).

symbolism of his sword, shield, and liquor pure.[6] Though in books 1 and 2 he seems a Christlike redeemer, he never in the six completed books receives Christian training, a reform we might have expected in the epic's unwritten latter half.

Arthur's limited awareness brings passional turmoil: his dream of a fairy queen (*FQ* 1.9.6–16) inflicts a love-wound for a very mysterious beloved.[7] What is his relation to Tanaquill-Gloriana: will he be perfected by seeking and "marrying" her glory? If so, is it *worldly* glory that inspires his heroism, as Gordon Teskey argues, or is Jeffrey Fruen right in viewing Gloriana as a more complex and transcendent glory,[8] and is Spenser's sequence of virtues designed to draw Arthur to that glory?

---

[6] On Arthur's arms, and their disparity from Ariostan romance and from Redcrosse's "armor of God," see A. C. Hamilton's annotations to *FQ* 1.7.29–36; Paul Alpers, *The Poetry of The Faerie Queene* (Princeton: Princeton Univ. Press, 1967), 166–79; James Nohrnberg, *The Analogy of "The Faerie Queene"* (Princeton: Princeton Univ. Press, 1976), 207, 273–76, 301–2, 362 et passim; Douglas Brooks-Davies, *Spenser's* Faerie Queene: *A Critical Commentary on Books I and II* (Manchester: Manchester Univ. Press, 1977), 74–79; Michael Leslie, *Spenser's "Fierce Warres and Faithfull Loves": Martial and Chivalric Symbolism in "The Faerie Queene"* (Cambridge, UK: D. S. Brewer, 1983), 49–56, 104–32; Kenneth Gross, *Spenserian Poetics: Idolatry, Iconoclasm, & Magic* (Ithaca, NY: Cornell Univ. Press, 1985), 58–59, 129, 134–40, 143, 152; Darryl J. Gless, *Interpretation and Theology in Spenser* (Cambridge, UK: Cambridge Univ. Press, 1994) 54–55, 62–70, 98–99, 115–17, 127–33, 188–89; and Darryl J. Gless, "armor of God," *Spenser Encyclopedia*, ed. A. C. Hamilton et al. (Toronto: Univ. of Toronto Press, 1990).

[7] The poem's fairy symbolism and pagan theophanies, notably Cupid's role in causing Arthur's quest, veils the poem's Christian-Platonic allegory which (as in *The Fowre Hymnes*) would be unveiled in the poem's final half, disclosing Gloriana's fullest meaning.

[8] Gordon Teskey, "Arthur in *The Faerie Queene*," *Spenser Encyclopedia*, ed. A. C. Hamilton et al. (Toronto: Univ. of Toronto Press, 1990); Jeffrey P. Fruen, "'True Glorious Type': The Place of Gloriana in *The Faerie Queene*," *Spenser Studies* 7 (1987): 147–73; Jeffrey P. Fruen, "The Faery Queen Unveiled? Five Glimpses of Gloriana," *Spenser Studies* 11 (1994): 53–88. Cf. "Gloriana" in Nohrnberg, *Analogy*, and David Lee Miller, *The Poem's Two Bodies: The Poetics of the 1590 Faerie Queene* (Princeton, NJ: Princeton Univ. Press, 1988).

Disrupting these iconic issues, a darkness looms in the sources: did Spenser intend to subject Arthur to impurities as troubling as those in Malory's anthology? In 1997 *Arthuriana* debated "Adultery in Arthurian Romance," and Cherewatuk's *Marriage, Adultery, and Inheritance in Malory's Morte Darthur* (2006) holds that "Adultery lies at the heart of the Arthurian tragedy."[9] Of the many adulteries in Malory, three of them pointedly threaten Arthur's moral and political stature.[10] How did Spenser deal with them?

Adultery # 1. Uther Pendragon Assails Queen Igrayne, Wife of King Gorlois: The Birth of Arthur

Arthur's conception is far from immaculate, as Merlin's trickery enables Uther, disguised as Gorlois, to sleep with Igrayne.[11] Spenser skirts this key adultery. Though he mentions Uther four times, Igrayne once, and Gorlois once,[12] he omits the story of Uther's raging lust for Igrayne when she and Gorlois visit, her refuge at Tintagel as the kings battle, and Merlin's role in transforming Uther to look like Gorlois (recalling Jove's trickery that begat Hercules on Alcmena).[13] Both Geoffrey of Monmouth and

---

[9] *Marriage, Adultery, and Inheritance in Malory's "Morte Darthur"* (Cambridge, UK: D. S. Brewer, 2006), 56. Cf. Catherine Batt, "Malory and Rape," *Arthuriana* 7, no. 3 (1997): 78–99.

[10] French sources assume the adulteries, and Scots chroniclers use them to demean Arthur's rule, but Geoffrey and Malory revise them to keep Arthur's authority intact, and even to enhance it.

[11] See Rosemary Morris, "Uther and Igerne: A Study in Uncourtly Love," *Arthuriana* 4 (1985): 70–92.

[12] Uther is in Eumnestes's chronicles (2.10.67, 68) and Merlin's prophecies (3.3.52, 55), Igrayne in the Letter to Ralegh, and Gorlois in Merlin's prophecies (3.3.27). Gorlois and Igrayne parented not only Morgause but also Artegall, Arthur's "salvage" half-brother.

[13] Plautus, *Amphytrion*. On Merlin's amendment by Geoffrey, Malory, and Spenser, see William Blackburn, "Spenser's Merlin," *Renaissance and Reformation* n.s. 4 (1980): 179–98; William Blackburn, "Merlin," *Spenser Encyclopedia*, ed. A. C. Hamilton et al. (Toronto: Univ. of Toronto Press, 1990); Patrick Cheney, "'Secret Powre Unseene': Good Magic in Spenser's

Malory give full accounts, ameliorating Uther's adultery by Merlin's prophetic magic and his negotiating to take and educate the child. Spenser includes but revises this important detail: his Merlin entrusts the training to newly invented Timon, whose name means "honor"[14] and who no doubt resembles the Reformation sages who taught Spenser at Merchant Taylors' School. To alert readers to his cleansing of Arthur's origin, Spenser twice uses *narratus interruptus*. The caesura that ends the Briton chronicles (2.10.68) politely erases Arthur's seamy birth by Merlin's trickery. Spenser's Reformed Merlin shapes a nobler Arthur by enlisting Timon and by crafting supernatural arms, but Merlin's prophetic skill is not displayed until book 3 where he foretells the triumphant dynasty of chaste Britomart. That Merlin breaks his account in a "suddein fit" (3.3.50) may show anxiety about Elizabeth I ending Tudor rule, but like the caesura in Eumnestes's chronicle it also underscores Spenser's ability to reshape history into allegorical myth. He improves history by showing "*what might best be*," avoiding flaws in geniture that would mar his *summa ethica* to celebrate Tudor rule. Geoffrey and Malory had begun to justify the adulteries, but Spenser went further, transforming Malory's Arthurian tragedy into epic exaltation.

Adultery # 2. Arthur Seduces Queen Morgause, Wife of King Lot: The Birth of Mordred

Arthur's image is directly stained when King Lot sends his lovely wife Morgause, along with their four sons (including Gawain), to spy on the newly crowned Arthur. Since neither Arthur nor Morgause knows they are half-siblings, he ardently

---

Legend of Britomart," *Studies in Philology* 85 (1988): 1–23; Matthew A. Fike, "Spenser's Merlin Reconsidered, *Spenser Studies* 13 (1999) ed. A. Prescott and T. P. Roche Jr., 89–99; Matthew A. Fike, *Spenser's Underworld in the 1590 "Faerie Queene"* (Lewiston, NY: Edwin Mellen Press, 2003), "Merlin's Ambiguous Hell Power in Book III," 85–96.

[14] Nohrnberg, *Analogy*, 717. Timon, if he resembles the Reformation teachers at Merchant Taylors, would be more disciplined than Merlin, who nevertheless visits the tutorial regularly.

courts her for two months, and she agrees to sleep with him. In sharp contrast to Lady Igrayne, who fled from Uther's lust and had to be tricked into adultery, Morgause, as Dorsey Armstrong explains, submits to lechery and thus contributes significantly to their monstrous offspring.[15] Merlin is not involved except to tell Arthur the next morning of the incest and of begetting a babe who will destroy his reign. Arthur orders a Mayday slaughter of innocents, putting every newborn boy on a pilotless ship. All drown except Mordred, who later joins Agravain in spying on Guenevere and Lancelot, splitting Arthur from his queen and greatest knight. In *The Alliterative Morte Arthure*, when Arthur leaves to conquer Rome, Mordred engineers disaster: he usurps the throne, incestuously marries and begets children on the formerly barren Guenevere, and exchanges death-blows with his father at Salisbury Plain. British chroniclers ameliorate even this disastrous adultery by analogy with David and Bathsheba,[16] and with Charlemagne's begetting of Roland, in keeping with the use of royal incest tales to promote confession in the twelfth and thirteenth centuries.[17] Spenser, however, does not invoke such analogies; nowhere does he hint at Arthur's future fling with Morgause and the fatal birth of Mordred.

---

[15] Dorsey Armstrong, "Malory's Morgause," in *On Arthurian Women: Essays in Memory of Maureen Fries* (Dallas: Scriptorium Press, 2001), 149–60. We note that King Lot is as culpable as his wife for this fatal adultery. The simple contrast of Morgause's lust and Igrayne's chastity is overshadowed by the astonishing complexity of Guenevere's "trew love" and its "good end."

[16] M. Victoria Guerin, "The King's Sin: The Origins of the David-Arthur Parallel," in *The Passing of Arthur: New Essays in Arthurian Tradition* (New York: Garland, 1988), 15–30; David Scott Wilson-Okamura, "Adultery and the Fall of Logres in the Post-Vulgate *Suite du Merlin*," *Arthuriana* 7, no. 4 (1997): 16–46.

[17] Elizabeth Archibald, "Arthur and Mordred: Variations on an Incest Theme," *Arthurian Literature* 8 (1984): 1–27.

Adultery # 3. Lancelot's Affair with Queen Guenevere and with her Displacement, Elaine of Corbin: The Birth of Galahad

Besides hiding the adulteries that shade Arthur's birth and death, Spenser's most striking omission is the grandiose adultery of Lancelot and Guenevere. This one fully challenges Arthur's moral authority—partly by its complicity with Arthur's power and partly by its entanglement with the grail-quest, which, oddly enough, is set in motion by a "holy adultery."

Malory defines the greatness and the tragedy of Arthur's reign by stressing the complex depth of Lancelot and Guenevere's bond. Unlike other adulterers, they do not seek to displace or discredit a royal spouse. Indeed they love Arthur and persistently magnify his "worship" in Round Table fellowship. Malory defuses the French sources' bleak judgment of their bond by praising the love during Arthur's rule:

> nowadays men can nat love sevennyght but they muste have all their desyres. [. . .]. Thy sys no stabylyte. But the olde love was nat so. For men and women coulde love togydirs seven yerys, and no lycoures lustis was betwyxte them, and than was love trouthe and faythefulnes. And so in lyke wyse was used such love in kynge Arthurs dayes. (1120; XVIII.25).[18]

During his long and ardent homage to Guenevere, Lancelot is pursued by many women—crafty queens like Morgan le Fay and ardent virgins like the two Elaines. He sternly resists them all. But Elaine of Corbin and her father Pelles mimic the ruse that begat Arthur; they dupe Lancelot into begetting Galahad, best knight of the Grail. Elaine drugs Lancelot and pretends to be Guenevere calling him to her bed, so he impregnates her with a "holy bastard." Beverly Kennedy argues that this event induces the first "real adultery" between

---

[18] Malory, *Works*, 1120; XVIII.25. See Robert S. Sturges, "Epistemology of the Bedchamber: Textuality, Knowledge, and the Representation of Adultery in Malory and the Prose *Lancelot*," *Arthuriana* 7, no. 4 (1997): 47–62.

Lancelot and Guenevere.[19] It devastates their friendship, causing Guenevere's intense jealousy and Lancelot's two-year madness, then festers into a dark mode of adultery that destroys Round Table unity. Spenser entirely omits this compelling drama; *The Faerie Queene* never mentions these key figures in Malory: Lancelot and Guenevere, Elaine and Pelles the fisher-king, Galahad and the Grail.[20]

How can Arthur attain mythic grandeur without the beautiful, majestic Guenevere? Studies by Beverly Kennedy, Edward Donald Kennedy, Karen Cherewatuk, Geraldine Heng, and Kenneth Hodges help us realize the importance of Arthur's queen: she affirms his greatness with her dowry of a Round Table and a hundred knights, added to his mere fifty; then she manages the brilliance of his court with a dimension of enchantment that captivates Lancelot and every reader.[21] Spenser sweeps us so raptly into his epic fairyland that we miss how radically he has changed Arthur's story—linking him not to Guenevere, nor to a lady of the lake, but to Gloriana.

Gloriana and the Chastening of Arthur

Unlike the sensual Guenevere (whose name, *bright-wave* or *spirit-wave*, suggests Venus's erotic oceanic allure), Gloriana's chaste sapience definitively inspires the twelve virtues in her noble subjects,

---

[19] B. Kennedy, "Adultery in Malory's *Le Morte d'Arthur*," *Arthuriana* 7, no. 4 (1997): 63–91.

[20] Eumnestes briefly mentions Joseph of Arimethea. Could Spenser, in the final legends of *The Faerie Queene*, have devised a "Reformed grail-quest" for Arthur's fulfilment?

[21] E. D. Kennedy, "Malory's Guenevere: 'A Woman Who Had Grown a Soul,'" *Arthuriana* 9, no. 2 (1999): 37–45; B. Kennedy, "Malory's Guenevere: A 'Trew Lover,'" in *On Arthurian Women: Essays in Memory of Maureen Fries*, ed. Bonnie Wheeler and Fiona Tolhurst (Dallas: Scriptorium Press, 2001), 11–34; Cherewatuk, 24–55; G. Heng, "Enchanted Ground: The Feminine Subtext in Malory," in *Courtly Literature: Culture and Context*, ed. Keith Busby and Erik Kooper (Amsterdam: John Benjamins, 1990), 283–300; K. Hodges, "The Death of Guinevere" in *Forging Chivalric Communities in Malory's "Le Morte Darthur"* (New York: Palgrave Macmillan, 2005), 129–53.

and collectively in Arthur. We noted that Arthur's Christlike acts are veiled in romance symbolism. Gloriana, with her many names and subtypes, her many layered meanings, is even more mysteriously veiled in "fairy" symbolism. Her advent as Tanaquill in a sensual dream-vision gives way to Gloriana's mystic spirituality, chastening Arthurian romance with doctrinal allegory, interweaving Malory's chivalric quests with Langland's spiritual pilgrimage and with the virgin's rose of light. In displacing Guenevere with Gloriana, Spenser not only exalts Elizabeth I by setting a transcendent goal for her to aspire to, but he also cleanses Arthur's legend of its troubling adulteries, drawing Arthur to the same mystic perfection.

Aware of the impurities in Geoffrey and Malory, Spenser portrays a young, not-yet-adulterated Arthur, preempting the moral flaws that so annoyed Ascham and Erasmus about Arthurian romance. Spenser withholds Uther's passionate adultery and Merlin's role in enforcing it, and he completely omits the monstrous Mordred and the horrific end of beautiful Morgause, beheaded by her son Gaheris when he finds her bedded with Lamoracke. (We note Spenser's remark, at the end of the Legend of Courtesy, that the "good" Pelleas and Lamoracke cannot quell the Blatant Beast's fury.)[22] As for the war on Rome, by which the *Alliterative Morte Arthure* connects Arthur's final delusion of greatness with Mordred's treachery, Malory cleverly moves that war near the start of the *Morte Darthur* to establish Arthur's incomparable greatness. Unlike Kent Hieatt, I do not see the Roman War as the model for *The Faerie Queene's* intended conclusion,[23] for Spenser's epic (like Dante's) moves beyond the glorifying of war toward mystic consummation.

---

[22] *FQ* 6.12.38. The Legend of Courtesy's reference to two of Malory's main knights, its many-tongued beast, and its focus on "salvage" aspects of human nature, form Spenser's major collective allusion to Malory: why at this point in *The Faerie Queene*? But he revises Malory's "Questing Beast" (spawn of incestuous adultery, with fuzzy shifting moral significance) to connote slanderous discourtesy—not a conclusive and comprehensive vision of evil. See Dorsey Armstrong, "Malory's Questing Beast and the Geography of the Arthurian World," in Armstrong and Kenneth Hodges, *Mapping Malory: Regional Identities and National Geographies in "Le Morte Darthur"* (New York: Palgrave Macmillan, 2014), 156–72.

[23] For David Scott Wilson-Okamura, *Spenser's International Style* (Cambridge, UK: Cambridge Univ. Press, 2010), *The Faerie Queene* must

Spenser has chastened Arthur in many ways—precluding all adultery in this young and noble prince, proclaiming his moral perfection in the "Letter to Ralegh," and depicting in books 1 and 2 his conquest of ultimate human debilities; but Spenser's Arthur is not yet perfect, just in process. Like the Redcrosse Knight he is subject to Calvinist abjection, steadily descending in the first half of his quest before discovering in the epic's second half (alas, unwritten) his full dependence on God's grace and on the chaste sapience of a female partner—whom he will "marry" only in a mystic sense. As in the moving conclusion of *Morte Darthur*, where Lancelot finally achieves spiritual reform by imitating Guenevere's arduous restraint, Spenser's Arthur would be drawn to a similarly arduous "perfection" (Malory's persistent term). To enable that goal, Spenser severely revised Geoffrey and Malory, transposing Guenevere into a figure resembling Beatrice and the Virgin Mary. Instead of an *Arthuriad*, an exhilarating *Glorianad* seeks to perfect an ancient mythic king and an early modern virgin queen.

How then could Spenser's final six legends have perfected Arthur, considering that in books 1–6 he descends into the confusions of a material body in a self-idolizing society? Books 1 and 2 (Holiness and Temperance) offer a Christlike "Reformation Arthur," who helps saintly Redcrosse and prudent Guyon in an *intellectual allegory* that omits the all-too-human Guenevere, dividing her into an exalted Gloriana and a demonic Duessa. Books 3 and 4 (Chastity and Friendship) heighten Arthur's confusion, for their *passional allegory* subordinates him to chaste Britomart, an archaic female warrior who is Gloriana's fullest "embodiment." Spenser even devises a female theology to inform Britomart's marriage-quest and her Trinitarian subtypes (Florimell, Belphoebe, Amoret), two of them with an immaculate sun-birth. That in these books Arthur is distracted by Florimell and displaced by Britomart gently nods at his adulteries in *Morte Darthur*. Books 5 and 6 show Arthur enduring deeper moral perplexity in the *sensory allegory* of Justice and Courtesy, with their materialist narrowing evident in Duessa, in Timias, in Turpine and the cannibalistic "Salvage Nation." In this schematic Christian-Platonic descent of books 1–6 the magnificent Arthur (like

---

end in war if it is to rival the epics of Homer, Virgil, Ariosto, and Tasso.

Redcrosse in cantos 1–6 of book 1) becomes morally paralyzed,[24] too sympathetic to Duessa in book 5, unable to eliminate Orgoglio's sibling Disdain in book 6. Spenser is aware of the shrinkage, distancing his heroes (and himself as poet) from the goals of book 1: faith in God, charity to all, joyous vision of God's saint-filled city.

No one has yet deciphered *The Faerie Queene*'s holistic design, the six additional legends needed for Arthur's full figuration;[25] but instead of envisioning Arthur as wholly perfect and providentially empowered from the outset, we should expect this prince to complete a full spiritual drama in the final half of Spenser's epic. When the once and future king returns, will he be Charles Williams's spiritual Galahad, immediately manifesting the perfection at which Spenser aims; or will he find glory only through a time of dreadful Calvinist abjection? In the *Alliterative Morte Arthure*, not long before facing Mordred's death-blow, Arthur dreams of a great bear locked in combat with a terrifying dragon.[26] As his helmet shows, Arthur like his father Uther holds the deadly dragon-power, but he is also the great bear, as his name "Arrrthur" implies.[27] Though

---

[24] See William A. Oram, "Spenserian Paralysis," *Studies in English Literature* 41 (2001): 49–70.

[25] See R. L. Reid, *Renaissance Psychologies: Spenser and Shakespeare*, forthcoming at Manchester Univ. Press.

[26] Karl Heinz Goller, "The Dream of the Dragon and the Bear," in *The Alliterative Morte Darthure: A Reassessment of the Poem* (Cambridge, UK: D. S. Brewer, 1981), 130–39.

[27] In "The Woman Who Married the Bear," beloved master-tale of many cultures, the bear's mythic profundity (a shaman with spiritual prowess) appears only to those who in maturing identify with it. *Arthur*, Welsh for bear, is, like *Beowulf*, a bear-king; Italy's *Arcadia* is an idyllic realm of noble bear-people, and *Ursa Major and Minor* are central constellations that hold the pole star. The protoroot of the creature's names (Italian *orso*, Latin *ursus*, French *ours*, Welsh *arth*, Greek *arktos*, Sanskrit *rksha*, British *bear*) is the snarling "rrrr." It veils its supernatural grandeur in the sordid world, shifting at dawn from lordly human to bestial bear, as in folktales. See Beryl Rowland, *Animals with Human Faces: A Guide to Animal Symbolism* (Knoxville: Univ. of Tennessee Press, 1973), 31–35; Joyce E. Salisbury, *The Beast Within: Animals in the Middle Ages* (New York: Routledge, 1994), 80–86, 158, 161–66; *The Woman Who Married the Bear: Versions of a Folktale* (Ottawa: National Museum of Canada, 1986); *The Practice of the Wild:*

the fantasy of Camelot (or Carbonek or Camlann) assumes a morally perfect ruler, Arthur is in mythic totality (as in the sum of his legends) a shape-shifting bear-king with an endless capacity for power and ugliness who, like the Redcrosse Knight, must ultimately struggle with a dragon of his own making. The name of Mordred, the monstrous child of Arthur's adultery, might derive from *merdraig*, sea-dragon.[28] Until we discern Spenser's ardent discourse with the disturbing primordial extremes of Malory's *Morte Darthur*, our understanding of Spenser's epic will remain rather shallow, with little for God and Gloriana to tame and contain.

Emory & Henry College

Essays by Gary Snyder (San Francisco: North Point Press, 1990), 155–74; "Three Drops of Blood," "White Bear Whittington," Beorn the bear-man in Tolkien, *The Hobbit*.

28 Goller, "The Dream of the Dragon and the Bear," 138.

Nationhood as Illusion
in *The Spanish Tragedy*

Emily Stockard

K AY Stockholder and Katherine Maus have argued that social status lies at the heart of *The Spanish Tragedy*, but a more pointedly political orientation reveals the concept of nationhood to be a particular focus of the play's anxiety.[1] Writing at a time when, as Richard Helgerson has shown, building national identity was a consuming concern of lawyers, voyagers, poets, and playwrights, Thomas Kyd portrays characters who act as if they serve a common national interest. In so doing, they enact a definition of nationhood that is, to use Helgerson's framework, "inclusionist," with a range of social groups afforded "privileged participation in the national community."[2] Within the framework of the revenge tragedy, however, Kyd includes a number of dramatic elements by which he emphasizes and then exposes as fiction the inclusionist assumptions about nationhood that initially motivate the actions of those in the lower rank.

Kyd opens with the figure of Andrea: this ghost, come from the grave, sets up the shifts in perspective that will follow. The play's premise begins with Andrea seeing himself as having fought

---

[1] See the Introduction to *Four Revenge Tragedies*, ed. Katharine Eisaman Maus (Oxford: Oxford Univ. Press, 1995), especially xvi–xviii, and Kay Stockholder, "The Aristocratic Woman as Scapegoat: Romantic Love and Class Antagonism in *The Spanish Tragedy, The Duchess of Malfi* and *The Changeling*," *The Elizabethan Theatre XIV*, ed. A. L. Magnusson and C. E. McGee (Toronto: P. D. Meany, 1996), 127–51.

[2] Richard Helgerson, *Forms of Nationhood* (Chicago, IL: Univ. of Chicago Press, 1992), 9.

valiantly against the Portuguese rebellion—the fictional war occasioned when Portugal resists its status as a tributary of Spain.[3] Given that he has recently lost his life in that endeavor, his initial view is remarkably circumspect: "For in the late conflict with Portingale / My valor drew me into danger's mouth / Till life to death made passage through my wounds."[4] Not yet in the revenging mood, Andrea views his death simply as the result of providing military service for the collective cause of Spain, which he has performed with "valor." Once he has received the proper burial rites, the only question to be answered is, given the requisite chivalric intertwining of love and war, whether he should be assigned the Elysian locale befitting a warrior or a lover. These roles are bound together in Andrea's

---

[3] My view of Kyd's use of Spain and Portugal accords with that set out by editor Philip Edwards: "Historically speaking, his play is sheer fantasy." As Edwards goes on to point out, Kyd's fiction portrays the rebellion of Portugal against the tributary status forced upon it by Spain; given that the historical viceroy of Portugal was Philip's appointee, his own nephew, "war between the two men is an absurd thought." See Introduction to *The Spanish Tragedy*, ed. Philip Edwards (London: Methuen, 1969), xxiv. I clarify this point because more recent scholarship has argued for particular ways by which the play invokes historical events, giving readings that ground the play in anti-Spanish sentiment. As a starting point, see J. R. Mulryne, "Nationality and Language in Thomas Kyd's *The Spanish Tragedy*," in *Travel and Drama in Shakespeare's Time*, ed. Jean-Pierre Maquerlot and Michèle Willems (Cambridge, UK: Cambridge Univ. Press, 1996), 87–105. Eric Griffin has written a cluster of essays extending this line of argument, often with a focus on Spain's empire-building: "Ethos, Empire, and the Valiant Acts of Thomas Kyd's Tragedy of 'the Spains,'" *English Literary Renaissance* 31, no. 2 (Spring 2001): 192–229; "Nationalism, the Black Legend, and the Revised *Spanish Tragedy*," *English Literary Renaissance* 39, no. 2 (Spring 2009): 336–70; "'Spain Is Portugal / And Portugal Is Spain': Transnational Attraction in the Stukley Plays and *The Spanish Tragedy*," *The Journal for Early Modern Cultural Studies* 10, no. 1 (Spring/Summer 2010): 95–116. Griffin also authored *English Renaissance Drama and the Specter of Spain* (Philadelphia: Univ. of Pennsylvania Press, 2009), with the salient chapter being "Thomas Kyd's Tragedy of 'the Spains,'" 67–96.

[4] Thomas Kyd, *The Spanish Tragedy*, ed. Philip Edwards (London: Methuen, 1969), I.i.15–17. All further quotations will be noted parenthetically.

formulaic understanding: his "duteous service" merits the noble Bel-imperia's "deserving love" (I.i.9). But this blithe belief that meritori-ous service to Spain will be rewarded is shown throughout the play to be illusory.

Kyd portrays Andrea's shifting perspective as the Ghost of Andrea and Revenge witness the unfolding events. Watching the King of Spain entertain Prince Balthazar of Portugal, the high-ranking enemy at whose hand he died, Andrea protests:

> Come we for this from depth of underground,
> To see him feast that gave me my death's wound?
> These pleasant sights are sorrow to my soul,
> Nothing but league, and love, and banqueting!
> (I.v.1–4)

On the one hand, the banqueting scene represents peace—presum-ably the wished-for conclusion to the war between Spain and Por-tugal. On the other hand, it is the ruling families that, if events go as planned, will benefit from this peace, while the cost of the war and, paradoxically, of the peace, is paid with the lives of those like Andrea.

Andrea's premature death—"Death's winter," as he initially describes it—did not result simply from the chance of war. Rather, the dice were loaded against him. Subsequent descriptions empha-size the inequity in battle—an inequity built along the lines of dif-ference in status. Andrea, we come to hear from Horatio, was slain not as a result of one-on-one combat with Balthazar, but rather was set on by Balthazar's henchmen. Only by "taking advantage of [Andrea's] distress" is the prince able to strike the killing blow (I.iv.24). By contrast, Balthazar, owing to his status as prince, is allowed to live, despite being defeated by Andrea's fellow country-man, Horatio. So while Prince Balthazar is shielded by his Spanish counterpart Lorenzo, those fighting on behalf of the ruling houses suffer the full violence of the battlefield. Reporting to the Spanish King, the General details these fuller horrors of the conflict, won at a cost of what he first characterizes as "little loss":

> Here falls a body scinder'd from his head,
> There legs and arms lie bleeding on the grass,
> Mingled with weapons and unbowell'd steeds,
> That scattering overspread the purple plain.
> (I.ii.59–62)

Later off-handedly numbered at "three hundred or a few more," such is the "little loss," the price paid by the soldiers who die in order to reinforce the tributary status of Portugal and so allow Spain to prosper (I.ii.7, 108). With the General's casual reference to the deaths of unnamed soldiers, Kyd highlights an instrumental view held of the lower social echelon: those belonging to it exist in order to benefit those of higher rank.

The benefits to Spain come to be defined only by the interests of its ruling house, interests that will be furthered by a dynastic marriage with the Portuguese house, recently the foe of the Spanish forces. To enforce this selective distribution of benefits, the violence moves from the battlefield to the Spanish court. At court, in the figure of the King of Spain, Kyd holds out the manipulative fiction of inclusionist nationhood, only to undermine the validity of this view. When we first see the King, he is scrupulous in the extreme when rewarding those who serve him well. To the victorious soldiers, he promises "Two ducats, and on every leader ten, / That they may know our largesse welcomes them" (I.ii.130–31). This sort of largesse, extended initially, as might be expected, to those who fought for Spain, plays out as well in the King's conversation with his Knight Marshall, Hieronimo. Speaking of Horatio's noble exploits in the war, the King assures the hero's father, "Nor thou nor he shall die without reward" (I.ii.100). Hieronimo too acts in accordance with his belief in his place within the nation. Of Horatio, he says, "long may he live to serve my sovereign liege / And soon decay unless he serve my liege" (I.ii.98–99). As for himself, Hieronimo assures the King that Horatio, "never pleas'd his father's eyes till now, / Nor fill'd my heart with overcloying joys" (I.ii.119–20). The King's response supports this understanding of merit rewarded: "it greatly pleaseth us / that in our victory thou have a share, / By virtue of thy worthy son's exploit" (I.ii.124–26). The "share" given by the King will be the monetary reward, Balthazar's ransom, emphasized later in the play.

In troubling contradiction to the hierarchical nature of an inclusionist national structure, the King's "largesse" extends not only to the Spanish soldiers, but immediately as well to the captured enemy, Prince Balthazar, whose doubtful merits he is quick to acknowledge even to the point of fawning. The Portuguese Prince is assured that, although held prisoner at the Spanish court, he will be "free from bearing any servile yoke." In justification of this treatment, the King points to Balthazar's deserving actions: "For in our hearing thy deserts were great, / And in our sight thyself art gracious" (I.ii.148–50). Presumably, the deserving actions referred to include the killing of the King's own soldier, Don Andrea, beset by Balthazar's henchmen, a battlefield death elsewhere described in less-than-honorable terms. Bel-imperia, who unlike her uncle makes distinctions in merit, calls Balthazar's killing of Andrea a "murd'rous deed" and poses the rhetorical question, "For what was't else but murd'rous cowardice, / So many to oppress one valiant knight, / Without respect of honour in the fight?" (I.iv.72–75). Of the members of the Spanish ruling house, Bel-imperia alone, in her recognition of merit, enacts an inclusive nationalism rather than the imperialist drive indicated by her name.

The King's propensity to give favorable attention to those whom his own soldiers have risked their lives to defeat increasingly disturbs assumptions of a common national interest. After rewarding both Lorenzo and Horatio for the capture of Balthazar, and doing so in a manner that accords with their difference in status, the King leaves the stage with lines that similarly emphasize the difference between the Spanish soldiers, whom he pays to fight, and the Portuguese Prince, whom he sees as a friend: "Now let us hence to see our soldiers paid, / And feast our prisoner as our friendly guest" (I.ii.196–97).

Kyd places the Spanish King at center stage in a pivotal scene constructed to reveal pointedly the insubstantial nature of the bond between King and Spanish courtier, superseded as it is by the strong bond between the ruling houses of Spain and Portugal. On the King's one hand, Hieronimo is positioned to make an appeal to right wrongs that have occurred within Spain (the murder of Horatio); on the King's other hand, the Portuguese Ambassador sets out the terms of the proposed dynastic marriage that will link Spain and Portugal. Hieronimo's call for "Justice, oh, justice to Hieronimo!" is met by the King's question, "Who is he that interrupts our business?" (III.xii.27, 30). The sense of the royal "our" is clear: the interrupted business is the solidification of aristocratic interests to which the King gives ear. The Ambassador brings news of the Portuguese Viceroy's strikingly unusual plan to give the crown to his son immediately should the marriage take place, a move that will raise the place of the Spanish King's niece Bel-imperia to that of Portuguese queen. The Viceroy's proposal is set forward together with its clear object:

> To knit a sure inexplicable band
> Of kingly love and everlasting league
> Betwixt the crowns of Spain and Portingale,
> There will he give his crown to Balthazar
> And make a queen of Bel-imperia.
>
> (III.xii.46–50)

Thus Kyd stages, simultaneously and side by side, the knitting of bonds between the crowns of Spain and Portugal at the expense of the ultimate dissolution of any bond between the King and his Knight Marshall.

When Hieronimo's view of nationhood collapses, and with it the assumptions that supported the war against Portugal, he redraws the lines of warfare to fit his corrected vision.[5] Hieronimo turns to fighting those, his social superiors, whom he now perceives as making war against his family. In framing his situation as warfare, he chooses a method appropriate for a fight against those who outrank him: "Nor aught avails it me to menace them, / Who, as a wintry storm upon a plain, / Will bear me down with their nobility" (III.xiii.36–38). Understanding that the patterns of alliance fall not along national lines but along lines of class or caste, he determines that his former dutiful service will now amount only to such pretended gestures as will further his mission. In other words, to

---

[5] C. L. Barber pursues my line of thought when he characterizes Hieronimo's revenge as being driven by "the feeling of outrage to sanctified social values," See Barber's *Creating Elizabethan Tragedy* (Chicago, IL: Univ. of Chicago Press, 1988), 146. The chapter, "Unbroken Passion: Social Piety and Outrage in *The Spanish Tragedy*," 131–63, sets out his reading. I see the play as radically skeptical of those very values that Barber identifies. True, Barber describes Kyd's work as "a play of protest grounded in a demonstration of the ruthless forces latent beneath the ideal of benevolent royalty sustaining a sanctified society—forces ready to destroy at need the new high middle-class servants of the state . . . when their rising fortunes challenged caste interest" (159). But he draws up short of pointing to the fundamentally manipulative force wielded by the ultimately illusory idea of a "sanctified society."

further his battle, he will participate in the pretense that turns the tables. By continuing to create what he now understands to be an illusion, he gains a strategic advantage over those he has come to define as his enemies. Hieronimo instructs himself, "thou must enjoin . . . / Thine eyes to observation, and thy tongue / To milder speeches than thy spirit affords, / Thy cap to courtesy, and thy knee to bow, / Till to revenge thou know when, where, and how" (III. xiii.39, 42–44). Hieronimo's recognition of the illusion in which he has been heretofore an unwitting participant gives him the upper hand in its creation and ultimately in its destruction.

It is, of course, Lorenzo, the King's nephew and the play's chief villain, who, as Kyd stages it, creates the block to Hieronimo's access to the King. In this capacity, Lorenzo embodies most forcefully the prerogative of the ruling houses against which Hieronimo now fights. The assumptions of class prerogative find in Lorenzo's actions their extreme but logical expression: the violence—unquestioned and casual—aimed at those below them in rank. By means of this very early Machiavellian figure, Kyd nakedly portrays the instrumentalism inherent in the view taken by the highest social echelon of all lower in social status. After setting up one servant to be executed for murdering another, Lorenzo baldly declares, "myself shall be my friend / For die they shall, slaves are ordain'd to no other end" (III.ii.118–19). "Slaves," in Lorenzo's view, exist to serve his own ends. This instrumental view of servants is analogous to the use of soldiers in warfare, wherein the lower die to further the gains of the highest rank, who are themselves protected.

Kyd also implies a parallel between Lorenzo's treatment of Pedringano and the King's system of rewarding good duty, in the form of money, to those of lower rank. When Lorenzo combines a threatened violence with an offer of wealth and so coerces Pedringano into betraying Bel-imperia, Kyd portrays the easy corruption and ultimately illusory nature of the meritocratic system. Pedringano first pretends to have no knowledge of Bel-imperia's esteem for Horatio, whereupon Lorenzo threatens him with death, thus forcing the answer that is then said to merit reward. Pedringano, although seeming to have little choice in the matter, declares with unintentional irony that the reward binds him to Lorenzo: "your honour's liberality / Deserves my duteous service, even till death" (II.i.96–97). This service, though, as Lorenzo reminds Pedringano, is due to the person most able to pay him—in this case Lorenzo rather than Bel-imperia: "Thous know'st that I can more advance thy state / Than she, be therefore wise and fail me not" (II.i.103–4). The "store of golden coin, / And lands and living join'd with dignities," offered by Lorenzo is a prize quite out of Bel-imperia's capability to offer. Of course, Lorenzo has no intent to make good on this promised wealth; the rewards on offer for service are patently illusory—empty promises signified very literally by the empty box that Pedringano assumes holds his pardon. Although it is more obviously the case as practiced by Lorenzo, both he and his uncle reward actions that serve their class interest, with "duteous service" as well as merit defined as the most powerful see fit. In Lorenzo's hands, the system has the additional advantage of turning those of lower rank against each other.[6] Thus Lorenzo has Pedringano betray Bel-imperia and then murder Serberine, Balthazar's servant. Lorenzo's sense of class prerogative justifies not only his manipulation and legalized killing of servants such as Pedringano, but easily extends as well to the murder of the Spanish war hero Horatio when that death furthers the ends of his house.

With the dynastic alliance planned between Spain and Portugal, Kyd adapts a common comic formula to devastating ends. According to this formula, once the blocking forces are removed communal harmony will be restored, emblematically represented by and sealed in marriage. But Kyd peoples this formula so as to emphasize, once again, the costs borne by those of inferior social rank so that their superiors may live in harmony. Horatio, the blocking figure, the impediment to the alliance between the ruling houses, is summarily removed—murdered in mocking fashion by Lorenzo and Balthazar, Horatio's rival in love. The justification for Horatio's murder is framed in terms of Balthazar's deserving to possess Bel-imperia as his beloved, rather than Horatio. Balthazar argues that his rightful place in Bel-imperia's heart has been usurped by means

---

[6] Kyd emphasizes the logic of this corruption yet again when he stages its operation at the Portuguese court. There Villuppo falsely accuses Alexandro of murdering Balthazar, not because he has any grudge against his rival courtier but in order to gain a reward: "not for Alexandro's injuries, / But for reward, and hope to be preferr'd, / Thus have I shamelessly hazarded his life" (III.i.94–96).

of Horatio's deceit, which "in her heart set him where I should stand." And he laments, "Die heart, another joys what you deserv'st" (II.i.129, II.ii.20). Balthazar's perception of Horatio as unworthy of Bel-imperia's love is purely a function of class status, and so the murder of Horatio proceeds according to the instrumental ideology of the aristocracy. Horatio has value for Spain only as he serves as an instrument of war against Portugal; having captured the Portuguese Prince, he is disposed of when he blocks the dynastic peace—a peace that will erase any difference between Spain and Portugal, as conceived in purely familial terms, a relationship proclaimed by the King: "Spain is Portugal, / And Portugal is Spain" (I.iv.132–33). Although the immediate context of the formula stresses the subservient position of Portugal as a tributary, the King quickly takes steps to erase this difference.

The terms of the alliance between Spain and Portugal, as set out by the King, stage very explicitly the erasure of national interest for which Andrea, Horatio, and soldiers on both sides assumed they were risking their lives. Kyd goes out of his way to arrange the King's plan so as to make no sense in nationalist terms. As the King has no son to inherit, the King's brother and then nephew would be next in line. Hieronimo himself refers to Lorenzo as "the hope of Spain" (III.xiv.140). Yet there is no objection to the fact that the King, in effect, gives away the crown from Spain to Portugal—to the yet unborn son of his niece and the newly crowned head, the Portuguese Balthazar.[7] Specifically, the King stipulates,

> in case the match go forward,
> The tribute which you pay shall be releas'd,
> And if by Balthazar she have a son,
> He shall enjoy the kingdom after us.
>   (II.iv.18–21)

---

[7] In a less emblematic, more character-driven argument, Maus suggests that Lorenzo ignores his individual interests so as to preserve the aristocratic order, now emptied of its assumed moral status, from would-be usurpers like Horatio who actually practice the virtues once associated with the noble class. See Katherine Maus, *Inwardness and Theater in the English Renaissance* (Chicago, IL: Univ. of Chicago Press, 1995), 59.

Immediately following the marriage, Portugal's tributary status, over which the war was fought, will be forgiven; upon the King's death, the heir of the Portuguese Prince will head the family dynasty. The terms of the alliance and the passing of the crown of Spain to the fruit of this dynastic consolidation trump the rights of Lorenzo and his father, Castile—rights that would represent purely Spanish rather than cross-national class interests. The fact that the King's plan ignores his Spanish kin and so makes little logical sense in political terms calls attention to its emblematic representation of the terms that Kyd intends to emphasize: the class solidarity that operates in this trans-national alliance between two families.[8] Once the families are married, the kingdoms are interchangeable, bearing out the King's initial formulation: "Spain is Portugal, / And Portugal is Spain" (I.iv.132–33).

From the perspective of Hieronimo and Bel-imperia, however, the peace that is brokered between Spain and Portugal is not a peace but a continuation of war: it represents class consolidation that only furthers the power that can be turned against them. Bel-imperia speaks in terms of warfare when she tells Lorenzo he is "no brother, but an enemy; / Else wouldst thou not have us'd thy sister so: / First, to affright me with thy weapons drawn, / And with extremes abuse my company" (III.x.25–28). She sees herself as being under siege by the implicitly violent power of class solidarity that Kyd sets up Lorenzo to represent explicitly. When Hieronimo and Bel-imperia join forces in revenge, they refuse to allow their status as instruments to be used in this effort of consolidation and literally fight against the power that makes them targets of violence. True, they willingly destroy themselves in the process, but the logic of their suicides dramatizes their realization that the social system has only an instrumental place for them. In effect, they take control of their roles, making of themselves instruments for revenge and then, their use at an end, destroy themselves.

---

[8] William Empson would object to understanding the King's actions in emblematic terms on the grounds that such a reading has "refused to let the politics be real," *Essays on Renaissance Literature, Volume Two: The Drama*, ed. John Haffenden (Cambridge, UK: Cambridge Univ. Press, 1994), 52.

With the suicides of Bel-imperia and Hieronimo, Kyd implies the impossibility for these characters of a social or relational identity that is acceptable to them. What sort of identity, then, if any, might Kyd be offering as an alternative? Perhaps an answer lies in Hieronimo's vow of silence, a vow he enforces violently, and in anticipation of torture, by biting out his tongue. In terms of narrative logic, the gesture is puzzling; critics have worried over the fact that Hieronimo refuses to explain himself to the King when he has already said everything the King would presumably want to know.[9] As in the case of the King's unusual plan for dynastic consolidation, Hieronimo's action can be understood in terms that are emblematic rather than narratively logical. Most obviously, the gesture is one of social protest, made to face down authority, as he himself explains when asked why he refuses to speak: "What lesser liberty can kings afford / Than harmless silence? Then afford it me: / Sufficeth I may not, nor will not tell thee" (IV.iv.180–82). In the course of the play, Kyd has staged the disappearance of Hieronimo's identity, as it had been constructed entirely in social terms: his social identities as father, husband, and as courtier in a hierarchically ordered inclusionist nation have all vanished. His battle against the political forces responsible for his son's death, a social function of a sort, has also come to an end. What does remain to Hieronimo is his ability to gesture towards resistance of power.

Yet Kyd has Hieronimo insist not only on this gestural identity of resistance, but also and more importantly, on an interiority inviolate to the invasions of power. With seemingly nothing left to hide, Hieronimo continues to insist "never shalt thou force me to reveal / The thing which I have vow'd inviolate" (IV.iv.187–88). Nowhere in the play, however, are there any hints regarding the nature of "the thing" that might be revealed. The absence suggests that the vanishing of socially constructed identities has left Hieronimo nothing to keep secret—that this posited interior is as yet an empty space. Because the substance of this interiority remains undefined, a matter of simple assertion, it differs fundamentally from the sort

---

[9] Edwards discusses the possibilities of corrupt copies and multiple versions with alternative endings (Introduction to *The Spanish Tragedy*, xxxiv–xl).

of secret-keeping (what Maus labels "machiavellian inwardness"[10]) exemplified by Lorenzo and even by Hieronimo himself as necessary stratagems in the war that they wage. The secrets that they keep in these instances have an identifiable content; by contrast, Hieronimo's insistence upon keeping his "thing" inviolate gestures towards an interiority, but one unfilled. Such an interiority, were it developed, Kyd seems to suggest, could constitute an identity disentangled from the claims of power and so free Hieronimo from his dependence for his identify upon the constructs that he unwittingly furthered.[11] As it stands, however, Hieronimo's interiority proves to be a merely latent rather than a realized alternative to his vanished identity. This empty interiority is more than a simple analogue to the empty pardon box. It is a corollary, a result of Hieronimo's initial belief in that box—emblem of a completely manipulative and ultimately illusory promise of membership in an inclusionary nationhood.

Hieronimo's actions in the political sphere can be read as symbolic as well, and perhaps as ultimately empty. By breaking the peace and thus estranging Spain and Portugal, he severs for the moment this specific opportunity for class alliance and forcibly reasserts, in a kind of parody, a return to the illusory construct first held by himself, Horatio, and Andrea, of nationhood. Kyd arranges the pattern of deaths to recreate this national division, whereby the royal houses of Spain and Portugal, both drastically reduced, are once again at odds, the aristocratic solidarity broken. The King of Spain lives on, but his nephew, niece, even his brother (in a death often seen as superfluous) all die, leaving him the lone representative of his house. The death of Balthazar leaves the Viceroy of Portugal alive to swear off any wish to league with Spain: "Spain has no refuge for a Portingale," he says and requests to be set sail with his dead son in an unmanned ship, enacting what is in effect a death wish (IV. iv.217). His presumed death would leave standing his brother Don Pedro, the lone Portuguese counterpart to the King of Spain, both

---

[10] Maus, *Inwardness*, 58.

[11] Maus, *Inwardness*, 70. Along similar lines, but in a different context, Maus argues that "for Kyd, the connection between a challenge to authority and a highly developed sense of personal inwardness is not accidental but absolutely intrinsic."

of whom, by implication, will be forced to look below them for any social bond.

Although Kyd portrays the "inclusionist" definition of nationhood to be an illusory construct, he does not then replace it with the alternative "exclusionist" form of nationhood—nationhood defined as excluding all but the highest rank. Rather, even more skeptically, Kyd stages a vision whereby the concept of nationhood is itself a means of manipulating those of lower rank into actions that promote only the interest of the highest echelon, regardless of nationality. Deaths of social inferiors, such as Don Andrea and Horatio, even Pedringano and Serberine, are necessary to enable aristocratic solidarity across national lines. When Kyd's revenger, incited by this realization, makes war on the ruling houses, the early modern drama, often characterized as commenting on shifting social paradigms, reveals in violent terms a fear that nationalist ideology, however nationhood might be defined, is merely so much stagecraft.[12]

Florida Atlantic University

---

[12] Maus, *Inwardness*, 66. Noting the play's "skepticism, even nihilism," Maus makes a parallel religious argument, referring to "the hollow promises of a Christianity *The Spanish Tragedy* both evokes and renounces."

The Wife of Bath and
All's Well That Ends Well

Lewis Walker

ALTHOUGH there has been much qualification of the "problem play" category for *Measure for Measure, Troilus and Cressida,* and *All's Well That Ends Well* (and sometimes *Hamlet*), critics have found the designation "too useful to abandon in approaching the untraditional, disturbing nature of these plays."[1] For *All's Well,* the problematic elements are legion and include "the counterpoint—or clash—between romance and prosaic reality," its "unsatisfying ending," its "generic anomaly," and "its deep-seated pessimism about human worth and power."[2] The contemplation of these and other matters has led critics to suggest, in addition to the play's undisputed primary source (Boccaccio's *Decameron,* day 3, story 9, as translated by William Painter in *The Palace of Pleasure,* novel 38[3]), a number of other sources, analogues, and parallels. In seeking to explain how the play "attempts to unite both the physical and the spiritual elements of human existence within a single structure of the imagination," Peggy M. Simonds, for example, examines several motifs relating to sexuality and the sacred represented

---

[1] Susan Snyder, Introduction to *All's Well That Ends Well,* by William Shakespeare, ed. Susan Snyder (Oxford: Clarendon Press, 1993), 16. Subsequent quotations of *All's Well* come from this edition and are cited parenthetically.

[2] Ibid., 17–18.

[3] *Narrative and Dramatic Sources of Shakespeare,* vol. 2, *Comedies (1597–1603),* ed. Geoffrey Bullough (London: Routledge, 1958), 375–96. Subsequent quotations of Painter's translation are to this edition and are cited parenthetically.

in five different texts that were "part of a common cultural context" for "Shakespeare and other creative artists of the period."[4] Maurice Hunt, in his detailed discussion of Helena and merit, foregrounds and elaborates on stories (also mentioned by Simonds) about bed tricks from Genesis.[5] Given the high likelihood that Shakespeare drew on the Chaucerian oeuvre for *Troilus and Cressida*, one of *All's Well*'s companion problem plays,[6] it is possible, even likely, that he returned to another part of the same source for material and stimulus when he found himself writing a drama about a range of issues relating to marriage, sexuality, merit, social class, and age—matters treated in complex and suggestive ways in the Wife of Bath's prologue and tale.

It seems clear that at the time he was working on *All's Well*, Shakespeare had been reading Speght's newly published folio edition of Chaucer (1598) to acquire materials for *Troilus and Cressida*. *Troilus and Criseyde* seems to have contributed a number of details to *All's Well*, including Helena's reference to the precious receipt, by which she cures the King and which her father "bade me store up, as a triple eye, / Safer than mine own two, more dear" (2.1.105–6).[7] If this kind of detail can be traced to Chaucer's *Troilus*, based on the appearance of similar phrases expressing similar ideas in a specific textual site, how much more might Shakespeare have absorbed from

---

[4] Sacred and Sexual Motifs in *All's Well That Ends Well*," *Renaissance Quarterly* 42, no. 1 (1989): 33.

[5] Maurice Hunt, "Helena and the Reformation Problem of Merit in *All's Well That Ends Well*," *Religion and the Arts* 7, nos. 1–2 (2003): 144–45.

[6] See E. Talbot Donaldson, *The Swan at the Well: Shakespeare Reading Chaucer* (New Haven, CT: Yale Univ. Press, 1985); Ann Thompson, *Shakespeare's Chaucer: A Study of Literary Origin* (New York: Barnes & Noble, 1978); Lewis Walker, "Chaucer in Shakespeare: The Case of *The Nun's Priest's Tale* and *Troilus and Cressida*," *Upstart Crow* 15 (1995): 48–60.

[7] The connection is suggested by Howard C. Cole, *The "All's Well" Story from Boccaccio to Shakespeare* (Urbana: Univ. of Illinois Press, 1981), 3. The passage in Chaucer's *Troilus* comes in the middle of a lament by Criseyde that she did not flee with Troilus before she was forced to go to the Greek camp. She should have followed Troilus's advice, but "Prudence, allas, oon of thyne eyen thre / Me lakked alwey" (Geoffrey Chaucer, *Troilus and Criseyde*, in *The Riverside Chaucer*, ed. Larry Benson, 3rd edition [Boston: Houghton Mifflin, 1987]), V.744–45.

Chaucerian contexts whose entire structure constellates many of the themes of *All's Well* and dramatizes them as fully as it is possible to do in a narrative framework.[8] Not only did Chaucer—in the Wife of Bath materials—seem to anticipate a remarkable number of the issues Shakespeare was to explore in his play, but he also provided some specific hints about how the issues could be connected with each other and how they could be reconfigured to supplement and enhance the plot from Painter that he had in hand.

Among the notable characteristics of *All's Well* is its deployment and testing of proverbial language,[9] which is replicated on another level by the invocation and interrogation of formulas for fairy tale and romantic comedy.[10] The Wife of Bath, through her prologue and tale, does something quite similar, challenging traditional wisdom, be it in written or proverbial form. From the first words of her prologue, she mounts an assault on "auctoritee," reprocessing it as experience, and setting up text to be "glossed from one meaning into its opposite."[11] Her opening series of examples takes us on a wild ride through scripture, starting with the lesson she was told to take from the account of Christ's appearance at the wedding in Cana of Galilee: that she should be wedded only once (III.9–14). This is followed by the story of Christ's interview with the Samaritan woman at the well, which includes his revelation that she has had five husbands; the Wife professes not to understand, although it would seem to have an obvious application to her own case (III.14–25). Finally, she cites the scriptural injunctions "to wexe and multiplye" (III.28) and "to lete fader and mooder and take to me" (III.31). The Wife, then, takes a traditional gloss on the Cana story that bids her to marry only once, cites an example that she proves to be inconclusive on the matter of how many husbands she can have, refers

---

[8] Helen Cooper, *The Canterbury Tales*, Oxford Guides to Chaucer (Oxford: Clarendon Press, 1989), 153.

[9] Ira Clark, "The Trappings of *All's Well That Ends Well*," *Style* 39, no. 3 (2005): 281.

[10] Snyder, Introduction to *All's Well*, 9–10.

[11] "The Wife of Bath's Prologue," *The Riverside Chaucer*, III.1. Subsequent references to the "Wife of Bath's prologue and tale and to the "General Prologue" of *The Canterbury Tales* are to this edition and are cited parenthetically by fragment and line number(s).

to two more texts not especially relevant to this specific issue, and triumphantly concludes that there are no authoritative restrictions on her in this regard. Her skill at giving voice to conflicting authorities is taken to an even higher level when she quotes her past self ("But herkneth how I sayde" [III.234]) quoting her first three (old) husbands, to whom she imputes aphoristic wisdom about women and marriage that is then refuted by the appeal of her past self to her own feelings. An example comes in a short passage laden with proverbs: III.278–81. The Wife assumes the voices of her old husbands, asserting a kind of playwright's control over them, answering their supposed complaints, and even reporting what words she tried to put into their mouths:

> "Thou sholdest seye, 'Wif, go wher thee liste;
> Taak youre disport; I wol not leve no talys.
> I knowe yow for a trewe wyf, dame Alys.'"
>
> (III.318–20)

The imprisonment of the proverbial in a context where it has to contend with a stubborn reality, where it can be overridden by another voice, is a signal mark of *All's Well*. An especially rich example can be found in the Clown's attempt to teach the Countess a courtly answer that "will serve all men" (2.2.13–14). His first attempt to validate the answer is based on a proverb about the barber's chair "that fits all buttocks" (2.2.17). As he proceeds, he generates all sorts of proverb-like comparisons about the suitability of his answer, concluding with two that are variations on known proverbs:[12] the answer is as fit "as the nun's lip to the friar's mouth; nay as the pudding to his skin" (2.2.26–27). Once his all-purpose answer—"O Lord, sir!" (2.2.41)— is revealed, the Clown demonstrates, by answering the Countess's questions, how flexible it can be in sustaining the typical courtier in his evasiveness. But its value is undercut when the Countess decides to shift the ground for the phrase's putative use from what a courtier says to avoid getting into trouble to what he (or perhaps the Clown himself) might say while he is being whipped: "Indeed your 'O Lord, sir!' is very sequent to your whipping" (2.2.52–53). The Countess has stripped away the context wherein the phrase can be used to *prevent* difficulties and substituted one in which it is used *in response* to

---

[12] Snyder, 120.

("sequent to") punishment. The Clown acknowledges that "O Lord, sir," however authorized by aphoristic comparisons, fails him when it is confronted by the situation he is actually in (a humble servant in a great household) instead of the situation he imagines for himself (a courtier in a very different setting). His recognition that "I never had worse luck in my life in my 'O Lord, sir!' I see things may serve long, but not serve ever" (2.2.55–56) can stand as an epigraph for the play's handling of proverbial wisdom and, on a larger scale, for its appropriation of the genres of folk tale and romantic comedy. Shakespeare's subversions of generic convention have been variously registered. According to one critic, he "has taken a fairy-tale and made of it a morality."[13] In another account, "the play constantly derails narrative expectations and promises endings that turn out to be mirages."[14] We may return to Chaucer here to remark on the challenge offered by the Wife's prologue to conventional ideas of prologue; like *All's Well*, it can be said to put the audience on a false scent about its literary category, making us aware of "[T]he very impossibility of assigning the piece to the safe pigeonhole of a recognized genre."[15]

If the Wife of Bath's treatment of proverbial expression and the generic instability of her prologue might have attracted and stimulated Shakespeare, the potential for dramatic development of her performance—and the specific subjects she treats—would have given him further impetus. To the voices of her earlier self and those (actual and imputed) of her old husbands, we may add those of her fifth husband, both as he quotes from his book of wicked wives and as he engages in dialogue with another version of her earlier self (III.627–828). In addition, there are the voices, in the Wife's tale, of the knight who is guilty of rape, the queen who assigns him the task of answering the question of what women desire most, and the old woman who provides him the answer that saves his life and then demands marriage as her reward.

---

[13] Geoffrey Bullough, Introduction to *All's Well That Ends Well*, in *Narrative and Dramatic Sources of Shakespeare*, vol. 2, *Comedies (1597–1603)* (London: Routledge, 1958), 386.

[14] Katharine Eisaman Maus, Introduction to *All's Well That Ends Well*, by William Shakespeare, in *The Norton Shakespeare*, gen. ed. Stephen Greenblatt, 3rd edition (New York: Norton, 2016), 2638.

[15] Cooper, *The Canterbury Tales*, 141.

Of all the personas the Wife exhibits, one that is perhaps most immediately relevant to *All's Well* is the current self that preaches against virginity. Having begun with her defense of multiple marriages, the Wife turns to an endorsement of marriage itself by undermining the arguments for universal virginity. Although she allows virginity for those who would live perfectly (III.111), she renounces it for herself, noting that it must be lost for the purposes of procreation: she uses the word *engendrure* three times (III.128, 134, 137) to set up the justification for enjoyment of sexual activity. At the same time, she devalues *virginitee* and *chastitee*. In the course of 100 lines during which she discusses these matters (III.62–162), she uses the word *virginitee* seven times, along with synonyms like *chastitee* and *maydenhede*. The density of these references would, I believe, have had a good chance of catching Shakespeare's eye and contributing to the similarly obsessive focus on virginity in *All's Well*. This is especially true for the discussion of the subject by Paroles and Helena in the first scene. Paroles uses the same argument for losing virginity that the Wife does: "Loss of virginity is rational increase" (1.1.129–30) and "Within ten year it will make itself two, which is a goodly increase" 149–50). Furthermore, Paroles echoes the Wife's point that "if ther were no seed ysowe, / Virginitee, thanne wherof sholde it growe?" (III.71–72) when he maintains that "there was never virgin got till virginity was first lost. That you were made of is mettle to make virgins. Virginity by being once lost may be ten times found" (1.1.130–33). This paradoxical argument by itself could have been found elsewhere by Shakespeare,[16] but the argument coupled with the fascinated reiteration of the word *virginitee* increases the likelihood that Shakespeare was moved by the Wife to this verbal blitz.

The case of Paroles raises the issue of how Shakespeare might have redistributed the Wife's many voices in his play. As one of the three major characters added to the source, Shakespeare's man of words certainly has much in common with the Wife in his garrulity. Helen Cooper refers to the "wealth of words" under which the Wife submerges "strict logic."[17] If we extend the field of our investigation

---

[16] See Simonds, especially the second text she cites as part of the cultural context for *All's Well*: "Proci et Puellae," a colloquy by Erasmus.

[17] Cooper, *The Canterbury Tales*, 152, refers to the "wealth of words" under which the Wife submerges "strict logic."

to the description of the Wife in Chaucer's "General Prologue," we notice that, like Paroles, "in felaweshipe wel koude she laughe and carpe" (I.474). Moreover, there is a moment at the end of her prologue when her verbosity prompts a comment by the Friar:

> The Frere lough, whan he hadde herd al this;
> "Now dame," quod he, "so have I joye or blis,
> This is a long preamble of a tale!"
> (III.829–31)

This not only reinforces the impression of her loquacity; it provides testimony about it from a persona other than herself within Chaucer's narrative—much as Shakespeare's use of the name Paroles, and the comments of observers like Lafeu, furnish "independent" confirmation of the character's primary trait.

Paroles has something else in common with the Wife: a penchant for questionable travel. The "General Prologue," of course, inventories the holy sites she has visited (I.463–666), and notes that "She koude muchel of wandrynge by the way" (I.467). This means that she knows a great deal about straying from the beaten path, and it is hard to escape the impression that the wandering is moral as well as physical. Her account of traveling while her fourth husband was out of town confirms that she has never been concerned with the spiritual significance of any destination. As she puts it,

> I hadde the bettre leyser for to pleye,
> And for to se, and eek to be seye
> Of lusty folk."
> (III.561–63)

With this preface, she launches into a catalogue of the religious events she attended or participated in for secular purposes:

> Therfore I made my visitaciouns
> To vigilies and to processiouns,
> To prechyng eek, and to thise pilgrimages,
> To pleyes of myracles, and to mariages
> And wered upon my gaye scarlet gytes.
> (III.555–59)

Shakespeare's recollection of the Wife's obsessive peregrinations could be embedded in Paroles's dedication to restless motion, always away from responsibility. At the conclusion of his initial encounter with Helena, she chides him for being born under Mars when he was "retrograde" because "You go so much backward when you fight" (1.1.200, 202). The conversation continues this focus on Paroles's locomotion. He claims that he goes "backward" for "advantage," to which Helena retorts, "So is running away" (1.1.203–4). Paroles then contemplates his next trip, from which "I will return perfect courtier" (I.1.209). Not only is he an undertaker of questionable travel for himself; he is also the cause (or at least the enabler) of such travel in others. When Bertram proposes to go to "The Tuscan wars" (2.3.274) to avoid bedding Helena, Paroles chimes in with "To th' wars!" (2.3.276) and follows up with this elaboration:

> To th' wars, my boy, to th' wars!
> He wears his honour in a box unseen
> That hugs his kicky-wicky here at home,
> Spending his manly marrow in her arms
> Which should sustain the bound and high curvet
> Of Mars's fiery steed. To other regions!
> France is a stable, we that dwell in't jades.
> Therefore, to th' war!
>
> (2.3.279–86)

Although Paroles differs from the Wife of Bath in the specific reason he gives for this travel, he shares with her a distaste for staying at home and participating in routine, sanctioned marital activities. His predilection for foreign regions is especially reminiscent of the Wife. His counsel to Helena to "get thee a good husband" (1.1.216) seems to be contradicted by the spirit of his advice to Bertram to flee marriage, but like the Wife he is not much concerned with consistency. For him, as for her, motion is everything.[18]

---

[18] It should be noted that the Wife's dedication to travel both foreign and domestic—and the pilgrimage of sorts engaged in by the knight in her tale—may have influenced Shakespeare in ways beyond the construction of Paroles. The King, who in Painter appears in only one place, Paris, in *All's Well* is said by Helena to be at Marseilles (4.4.9), but when she arrives there to speak with him, she is informed that he has removed to Roussillon (5.1.28). Diana and her mother, the Widow, travel from Florence to Roussillon to assist Helena in the exposure of Bertram. Lavatch the Clown journeys from Roussillon to Paris and back again, and Lafeu, who

Lafeu discerns the illegitimacy of this modus operandi when he tells Paroles, "You are a vagabond, and no true traveller" (2.3.261–62)—which could be an echo of the Wife's "wandrynge." At two other points, Lafeu mentions Paroles in connection with travelers telling tales at dinner. In 2.5, he is musing aside while Bertram and Paroles are talking, and delivers himself of this opinion: "A good traveller is something at the latter end of a dinner, but one that lies three-thirds and uses a known truth to pass a thousand nothings with should be once heard and thrice beaten" (2.5.28–31). As with the Wife, dubious travel in Paroles is linked with unreliable wordiness. In the first onstage encounter between Lafeu and Paroles, the former explains how he came to see through the latter:

> I did think thee for two ordinaries to be a pretty wise fellow; thou didst make tolerable vent of thy travel, it might pass. Yet the scarves and bannerets about thee did manifoldly dissuade me from believing thee a vessel of too great a burden. I have now found thee. (2.3.203–7)

To the concentration in Paroles of words and wandering we can now add a third element, also found in Chaucer's Wife: overdressing. The Wife's account of her "visitaciouns," while her fourth husband was at London, cited above, ends by saying that she wore her "gaye scarlet gytes" to all of the ostensibly religious events she attended. As with the Wife, accounts of Paroles's movement seem inextricably linked to clothing. In his first interview with Helena, she tells him, "But the composition that your valour and fear makes in you is a virtue of a good wing, and I like the wear well" (1.1.205–7). This is, first of all, a judgment on his motion; that is, "his valor is

---

first appears with the King in Paris, also finds his way to Roussillon for the denouement. Bertram, of course, leaves home for Paris, steals away to Florence, and then returns to Roussillon, though curiously we do not see him arrive. When he does appear, it is at the summons of the King (5.3.25–27, 31), who expresses a desire to forgive him. It is as if Bertram is not really at home yet and must face a reckoning for his refractory wandering before settling in. This restlessness of the characters is matched by the dynamic of the play itself. As Maus points out, it is full of "aborted endings, continual deferrals, unanticipated reemergences, and surprising persistences," which "make the actual end of the play seem rather arbitrary" (Introduction to *All's Well*, 2638).

easily brought into accord with his fear, which dictates running to safety."[19] Helena then uses a metaphor for his rapid flight ("a good wing") that likely alludes to clothing (wing as a "shoulder lappet"[20]), and ends by extending the image with "wear."

Focusing even more tightly on the Wife's apparel, we note the assertion in the "General Prologue" that "Hir coverchiefs ful fyne weren of ground" and that the weight of such coverings on her head every Sunday amounts to ten pounds (I.453–55). The narrator then passes on to an inventory of, among other things, the numerous sites of pilgrimage she has visited. After this, he returns, as if unable to avoid it, to a consideration of her headgear. This time, instead of expressing its excessive nature by weight, he employs size for the same purpose, remarking that she has "on hir heed an hat / As brood as is a bokeler or a targe" (I.470–71). This fascination with adornment of the head could be partially responsible for Shakespeare's emphasis on Paroles's scarves, if we understand at least some of the latter to be "tied round the hat"[21] and if we imagine the Wife's "coverchiefs"[22] as analogous. A more direct transposition by Shakespeare involves the Wife's hose "of fyn scarlet reed, / Ful streite yteyd" (I.456–57), which seems to have prompted him to exhibit Paroles with outlandish sleeves; as Lafeu amusedly asks, "Why dost thou garter up thy arms o' this fashion? Dost make hose of thy sleeves?" (2.3.250–52). We might remark here that Chaucer's word "hosen" has made the transition to Lafeu's description virtually unchanged. And the tight lacing of the Wife's leggings (a kind of gartering) has migrated to Paroles's arms.

In any case, each form of the Wife's extravagance feeds into others, indeed seems to make the others inevitable. And the three emphasized here—locomotive, verbal, sartorial—are closely linked in ways that may have suggested to Shakespeare the virtual interchangeability of the same three excesses in Paroles. Lafeu, after his claim to have "found" Paroles through observing his clothes

---

[19] Snyder, 89n.

[20] Ibid.

[21] G. K. Hunter, ed., *All's Well That Ends Well*, by William Shakespeare, 3rd edition, Arden Shakespere (London: Methuen, 1967), 61n.

[22] Christine Ryan Hilary, explanatory notes to the Wife of Bath in the "General Prologue" of *The Canterbury Tales*, *The Riverside Chaucer*, 818.

(2.3.207), keeps coming back to this matter as the basis for his negative judgment. He calls Paroles a "window of lattice" (2.3.214), which refers not only to signs of lattice on taverns, but "openwork in clothes,"[23] thus using a metaphor inspired by the poseur's dress, indicating that he is easy to see through. Even when Lafeu wants to pursue a better relationship with Paroles and asks Bertram "to make us friends" (2.5.13), he cannot, when Paroles enters, forbear asking scornfully, "who's his tailor?" (2.5.16). And after making the distinction, cited above, between a "good traveller" telling stories at dinner and Paroles's blatant lying (2.5.28–31), he comments to Bertram, "The soul of this man is his clothes" (2.5.44–45). Lafeu's most comprehensive judgment on Paroles is expressed to Bertram's mother, the Countess, after Helena's "death" has been reported:

> No, no, no, your son was misled with a snipped-taffeta fellow there, whose villainous saffron would have made all the unbaked and doughy youth of a nation in his colour. Your daughter-in-law had been alive at this hour, and your son here at home, more advanced by the King, than by that red-tailed humble-bee I speak of. (4.5.1–7)

This passage may be missing something (there is no "if" clause to match the "had been"),[24] but Lafeu is clearly bringing together all three of Paroles's extravagances in one description. As far as clothing is concerned, "snipped-taffeta" refers to "silk slashed . . . to show the fabric underneath" as well as to "showy language"; taffeta is also associated with whores, reinforcing the notion of "show without substance"; and the "red-tailed humble-bee" with whom Paroles is equated is meretriciously flashy[25] (as well as providing a link to the Wife and her favorite color). The bee image adds unprofitable noise to frivolous dress. Finally, Lafeu's contrast of the evil that Paroles has wrought "there" (the misleading, both geographically and morally, of Bertram and the consequent death of Helena) with the benefits that would have accrued "here at home" without his baneful influence is based on an idea (perhaps derived from Chaucer's treatment of the

---

[23] Snyder, 133n.
[24] Ibid., 190n.
[25] Ibid.

Wife) that place is either good or bad depending on the intention with which one travels to it or leads others to travel to it.

The mention in Painter, *All's Well*'s primary source, of how the heroine, Giletta, travels to Florence "in the habite of a pilgrim" (393) was probably initially responsible for Shakespeare's resort to Chaucer. Given a plot focused on someone disguised as a pilgrim, where better to find material for elaboration than in a popular narrative, already familiar to the author, whose frame is a pilgrimage and one of whose characters is in large measure defined by her history as a pilgrim? One of the shrines visited by the Wife, "Galice at Seint-Jame" (I.466), the shrine of St. James of Campostella in Galicia, Spain,[26] probably furnished Shakespeare with the idea of having Helena identify herself as a pilgrim going to the same place; in her letter to the Countess, she says, "'I am Saint Jacques' pilgrim, thither gone'" (3.4.4), and later she appears in Florence bound, as she says, for "Saint Jacques le Grand" (3.5.34). This is "[p]robably Saint James the Great, whose shrine at Campostela was the most famous pilgrimage destination in Europe."[27] In Painter, Giletta simply becomes a religious pilgrim; no shrine or destination is mentioned.

The way that Helena joins with Paroles to metaphorize sexuality in terms of military activity shows a close association between sex and warfare akin to the Wife's recognition of her own aggressive eroticism. In her prologue, the Wife informs her listeners that

> For certes, I am al Venerien
> In feelynge, and myn herte is Marcien.
> Venus me yaf my lust, my likerousness,
> And Mars yaf me my sturdy hardynesse.
>   (III.609–12)

This comes after the Wife's account of her first four husbands and just before she describes her marriage to Jankyn the clerk, where her martial conduct in love is most in evidence: to express her disapproval of his book of wicked wives,

---

[26] Hilary, explanatory notes, 818; it should also be noted that the Wife, in her prologue, swears "by that lord that called is Seint Jame" (III.312).

[27] Snyder, 152n.

Al sodeynly thre leves have I plight
Out of his book, right as he radde, and eke
I with my fest so took hym on the cheke
That in oure fyr he fil backward adoun.
(III.790–93)

The Wife's violence in the name of love may have contributed, among other things, to Shakespeare's construction of the first set of exchanges between Paroles and Helena. It is significant that Helena initiates the use of military imagery to describe sexual campaigning: "You have some stain of soldier in you; let me ask you a question. Man is an enemy to virginity. How may we barricado it against him?" (1.1.113–15). Paroles develops the hints contained in this speech into a full-fledged analogy between the losing of virginity and the loss of a besieged city: "Virginity being blown down, man will quicklier be blown up. Marry, in blowing him down again, with the breach yourselves made you lose your city" (1.1.125–27). The paralleling of sexual and martial activity is unusually detailed here, with a series of terms involving blowing up, blowing down, breaches, and loss. It is as if the "Venerien" and "Marcien" aspects of the Wife have been given separate voices and are cooperating in this exegesis. Paroles's claim that he was born under Mars (1.1.194) indicates a possible link with the Wife's assertion that Mars is responsible for at least part of her nature.

That the subfield of military terminology drawn on in the conversation between Helena and Paroles has to do with siege is especially interesting in view of Shakespeare's name for his heroine, which he changed from Giletta (in the source) to Helena. Given the Clown's song about Helen as the cause of the sack of Troy, coming immediately after the Countess asks him to find her gentlewoman Helena (1.3.68–79), and given other details suggesting a Trojan connection for the play, it appears that Shakespeare has shaped his Helena as an ironic version of the original Trojan Helen. That is, the play's Helena is a sexual entrepreneur who leaves home to travel to a city to "take" it by curing the king and staking a claim to Bertram. Instead of allowing Paris (the son of King Priam) to take her, this Helena "takes" the city of Paris to find her love. My sense is that Shakespeare has filtered the heroine of Painter's story through the Wife of Bath's prologue and tale, making her more militant in her sexuality, and then added the ironic parallel to Helen of Troy for emphasis. The facts that Giletta in the source goes on pilgrimage as a way to remove herself from the Count's home so that (as she says) he can return, and that she encounters Beltramo (the original for Bertram) in Florence and is able to fulfill his seemingly impossible demands, Shakespeare took more or less straight from his source. But in his imagination he seems to have allowed this idea of pilgrimage in Painter to become attached at certain points to the Wife's story, which involves a history of going on pilgrimages as well as engaging in various other kinds of peregrination, because it reinforces the sense of Helena as a woman who ambitiously seeks out love. In her letter to the Countess explaining her sudden departure from Roussillon, Helena seems to regret her pursuit of Bertram and to vow penance:

> "Ambitious love hath so in me offended
> That barefoot plod I the cold ground upon,
> With sainted vow my faults to have amended."
> (3.4.4–7)

Whether Helena is sincere in her plan or not, her linking of pilgrimage with love, even if the former is a means of repudiating the latter, puts her in motion both geographically and emotionally—which in turn allows her again to take the initiative with Bertram. Indeed, throughout the play Shakespeare takes pains to intensify our sense of Helena as an active seeker of love. When she besieges Paris, persuading the King to submit to her ministrations, it is she rather than (as in the chief source) the King who proposes that she be rewarded with a husband of her choice if she succeeds.

Shakespeare, then, in reshaping and complicating a story about a woman who pursues love in the guise of a pilgrim, was drawn to the Wife of Bath, many strands of whose character he wove into his play. Much of what is morally questionable (though extraordinarily vivid and authentic) about the Wife is channeled into Paroles, who is thereby able to transcend the conventional figures of *miles gloriosus* and Vice that have been suggested as his prototypes.[28] Paroles,

---

[28] Alexander Leggatt, Introduction to *All's Well That Ends Well*, by William Shakespeare, ed. Russell Fraser, updated edition, New Cambridge Shakespeare (Cambridge, UK: Cambridge Univ. Press, 2003), 3, places Paroles in the tradition of "the braggart warrior," which "runs through

that is, is not simply a descendant of the Vice from the morality plays; he is the Vice in motion, plumed with spectacular finery and equipped with impressive (if meretricious) rhetorical skills. As such, he tends to deflect criticism from Helena,[29] who inherits the Wife's aggressive pursuit of love through pilgrimage, purged of its grosser elements.

To return to the Wife of Bath as a possible source for the interchangeability of the military and the sexual, we may note that the knight in the Wife's tale, "a lusty bachelor . . . saugh a mayde walkynge hym biforn," and "By verray force he rafte hire mayden-hede" (III.883, 886, 888). The uncontextualized violation of a generic virgin is very much like what Bertram seeks to accomplish with Diana of Florence. Despite his wooing of her, he obviously regards her as nothing more than a conquest ancillary to his war service. Shakespeare gives her a name (her model in the source is anonymous) that foregrounds her status as an exemplar of virginity.

Bertram is like the knight in other important ways, one of which involves his reluctance to consummate his marriage. The knight's complaints about being forced to wed the "olde wyf" (III.1046) who gave him the answer to the question of what women desire the most and thus saved his life, include this: she comes "'of so lough a kynde'" (III.1101). This is very much like Bertram's angry outburst about Helena to the King:

> She had her breeding at my father's charge.
> A poor physician's daughter my wife! Disdain
> Rather corrupt me ever.
>
> (2.3.115–17)

If Bertram seems to echo the knight's disdain, the knight's "loathly" wife argues for the value of "gentil dedis" as against "arrogance" that

---

the comedy of Greece and Rome, well into the Renaissance and beyond"; Philip Edwards, *Shakespeare and the Confines of Art* (London: Methuen, 1968), 110, identifies the Vice, Paroles, as one of the two cords pulling on Bertram (the other being his dead father); Helen Cooper, *Shakespeare and the Medieval World*, Arden Shakespeare (London: Bloomsbury, 2010), 122, maintains that *All's Well* "employs a morality structure" in which Paroles is "the Vice figure" who leads Bertram astray.

[29] Maus, Introduction to *All's Well*, 2640.

comes of "old richesse" (III.1170, 1112, 110) in much the same way that Helena asserts her own virtue, claiming Bertram as a payment for her service to the King (2.3.103–5) and persisting in her attempts to earn him through meritorious action.[30] The "olde wyf" of the tale, by her unknown origin and repulsive appearance, is as far removed from the knight's social realm as could be; she is an alien being. Shakespeare, in a similar spirit, increases the gap between the principals in his source, which has only Giletta come to Roussillon at the story's end to show how she has fulfilled Beltramo's conditions. In All's Well, Diana arrives first (5.3.157) to entangle Bertram in a web of lies and thus emphasize the bogus nature of his claim to "gentillesse." Helena then appears for the coup de grace. In other words, Shakespeare, having raised Bertram higher than Beltramo in the source, complicates the final scene by humbling him further than his prototype.

The possibility that Helena's discourse and actions with regard to her merit are partly derived from the "loathly lady" of the Wife's tale is strengthened by the linking, in both the tale and in All's Well, of age with the themes of sexuality and merit. More than one critic has noticed that Shakespeare has created an older generation that was not present in the original source, the members of which offer more or less sage advice to their juniors.[31] In particular, Bertram's mother the Countess is absent from Painter, and I think that her pronouncements about Helena's virtues may owe something to the tale's "olde wyf," whose reconstruction of what it means to have "gentillesse" involves the recognition that such a quality "cometh fro God allone" (III.1162) and that "he is gentil that dooth gentil dedis" (III.1170). In an observation that could be taken as a prejudgment of Bertram, the old wife notes that "men may wel often fynde / A lordes sone do shame and vileynye" (III.1150–51). Shakespeare's source in Painter does include a King, but he is developed very little, having nothing to say about the past and being absent from the final scene at Roussillon. The King in All's Well, however, makes it a point

---

[30] Hunt, "Helena and the Reformation Problem of Merit."

[31] Edwards, *Shakespeare and the Confines of Art*, 110; Maus, Introduction to *All's Well*, 2636; Sheldon P. Zitner, *All's Well That Ends Well*, Twayne's Critical Introductions to Shakespeare (Boston: Twayne, 1989), devotes a chapter to "Young and Old."

to express the wish, while remarking on the resemblance of Bertram's face to that of his handsome father, that "Thy father's moral parts / Mayst thou inherit too!" (1.2.21–22). He goes on to comment on the courtesy with which Bertram's father used those who were "below him" (1.2.41–45). His appearance at Roussillon in the final scene to supervise the exposure of Bertram shifts the power of judgment from Beltramo himself (in Painter) to the older generation that also includes Lafeu and the Countess. In this regard, the judgment scene is closer to that in the Wife's tale, where the knight is judged by the ladies of King Arthur's court, led by the Queen. The King's praise of Bertram's father sets up the Countess's later scathing apostrophe to her absent son:

> This is not well, rash and unbridled boy:
> To fly the favors of so good a king,
> To pluck his indignation on thy head
> By the misprizing of a maid too virtuous
> For the contempt of empire.
>
> (3.2.28–32)

Here we have a cluster of themes that Shakespeare would have encountered in somewhat different configurations in the Wife of Bath's prologue and tale: the rashness of extreme youth, the resistance to mature wisdom, and the repudiation of transcendent merit.

It is also worth noting that the Wife herself, in the prologue, may provide a model for the Countess's reflection on her own youthful passions. After treating at some length the ways in which she, as a *young* wife, dominated her three *old* husbands, Alice comes to her fourth, a "revelour" (III.453). She says nothing about his age, but it would seem, because of his behavior, that he is closer to her than the others were. Still, she seems to be claiming the advantage of youth when she remembers that she "was yong and ful of ragerye, / Stibourn and joly as a pye" (III.455–56). A few lines further on, she rejoices as she recalls her amorous adventures:

> whan that it remembreth me
> Upon my yowthe, and on my jolitee,
> It tikleth me aboute myn herte roote.
>
> (III.469–71)

The Countess's memories are not so joyful, but they are about the same subject matter. Thinking of the torments Helena suffers for love, she says, "Even so it was with me when I was young," calling love "this thorn" and admitting that sexual desire "is the show and seal of nature's truth, / Where love's strong passion is impressed in youth" (1.3.128, 129, 132–34). Though the Countess sees youthful love as more distressful than the Wife does, they both remember its ineluctability and its power.

The resemblances large and small between *All's Well* and the Wife of Bath material in *The Canterbury Tales* suggest that we should consider the possibility of a link between them. Talbot Donaldson distinguishes between substructure and infrastructure in studying the influences of Chaucer on Shakespeare. On the one hand, a substructure is a foundation that Shakespeare builds on, involving verbal echoes, similarities of detail, and thematic points of contact. Donaldson, for example, views "The Knight's Tale," "The Merchant's Tale," "The Tale of Sir Thopas," and the story of Pyramus and Thisbe from *The Legend of Good Women* as forming a substructure for *A Midsummer Night's Dream*. An infrastructure, on the other hand, while it does not provide the fundamental materials for building, does furnish "some of the important ways and means by which [Shakespeare] was enabled to build as he did." Donaldson regards the Wife of Bath as an infrastructure for Shakespeare's creation of Falstaff.[32] I would like to propose the materials related to the Wife in *The Canterbury Tales*, in all of their complexity, as both substructure and infrastructure for *All's Well*. It is intriguing to entertain the possibility that in shaping his primary source into a play, Shakespeare encountered another work that not only offered him much of the material he was to add, but also suggested ways in which he might add it.

University of North Carolina, Wilmington

---

[32] *The Swan at the Well*, 5.

A Necessary Evil: The Inverted Hagiography of Shakespeare's *Richard III*

Lainie Pomerleau

T HE popularity of William Shakespeare's *The Tragedy of King Richard III* owes as much to Richard's morally repugnant character as hagiographies of saints do to the saints' moral perfection. To mold the character of Richard, Shakespeare synthesizes medieval saints' lives and romances, creating a moral, instead of a purely biographical, truth. Almost never written within the saint's lifetime, hagiographies were offered as moral and spiritual exempla, and, later in the tradition, as an explanation for their sanctification. Saint veneration, while widespread throughout Catholic Europe and England, was almost always at heart a local affair, as communities often tied saints to their own histories and landscapes, like St. George and England or Thomas Becket and Canterbury. King Richard's malignant characterization actively engages English medieval hagiography, rich with saintly figures and their violent persecutors. *Richard III* is hagiographic in nature and operates as an adaptation of, not a break with, medieval hagiographic traditions established in works like William Caxton's *Golden Legend*, particularly his "Life of S. Thomas of Canterbury [Thomas Becket]," and the extreme conversion narrative of the romance *Sir Gowther*.

Saints' stories were part of medieval and early Tudor England's cultural fabric and were re-told and reenacted through religious services, drama, manuscripts, and early print. Saints' legends, ubiquitous and easily adaptable, adjusted to changing literary tastes as earlier martyr stories were reimagined through the lens of medieval romance. Even so, hagiography's conventions remained fairly stable: a miraculous or unusual birth and childhood, absolute devotion to the calling, sacrifice, martyrdom or physical suffering at the hands of evil or demonic forces, and the performance of miracles. Almost every saint also had a nemesis whose vicious ignorance complemented the saint's moral perfection. The victory of the saint's good over their enemy's evil was considered proof of holiness, and as medieval religious drama developed, tyrannical figures like Herod or Thomas Becket's King Henry II became, quite literally, "necessary evils."

Shakespeare's Richard III would, at first glance, appear another such tyrant, and his charmingly villainous character a foil to the redemptive figure of Richmond, later Henry VII, founder of the Tudor dynasty. Richard, whose body count includes two kings (Henry VI and Edward V) and two rightful heirs to the English throne (Edward, the Prince of Wales and son of Henry VI, and the other prince in the tower, also named Richard), seems at first another Herod waiting to be "out-Heroded." I suggest instead that Shakespeare's *Richard III* actually presents the audience with an adapted saint's life: the playwright's hagiographic treatment of an unholy, unblessed king results in a fully realized anti-hagiography. Shakespeare's *Henry VI*, part 3, and *Richard III* do not simply present the audience with an evil, ambitious king as proof of Richmond's goodness, but, like the Thomas Becket stories and plays before them, these dramas reenact Richard's rise and fall. Instead of merely presenting Richard as a raving tyrant or pagan persecutor, Shakespeare develops and presents a complete narrative of his biography and character. In a manner generically similar to a saint's story, we are shown the whole of Richard's adulthood and death. Unlike a saint, however, Richard is destined to fulfill the "promise" of his birth through lying, murder, and blasphemy.

There exists, for some, an uncomfortably close bond between professional early modern history plays and their distinctly popular predecessor, medieval drama. While not a tidy genealogy—English drama's "family tree" is as twisted and recursive as those of the Yorks and Lancasters—it seems needlessly shortsighted to claim that no connection existed between the two practices. While Shakespeare's plays are certainly hallmarks of Renaissance dramatic tradition, his and his audiences' experiences included memories of older forms, saint's plays and moralities. Helen Cooper observes that "we often label everything we like in the Middle Ages as proto-Renaissance, and everything we don't like in the Renaissance as medieval."[1] The effort to create neat boundaries has always been interrupted by Shakespeare's history plays, which often defy any type of neat classification. Efforts to simply label them as Tudor propaganda or political critique fall short, leaving the histories understudied or treated, much like medieval drama.

Perhaps part of the generic confusion derives from the titles and subject matter themselves; Shakespeare's histories were, at least in the medieval sense, tragedies. In the medieval tradition, tragedies are stories chronicling the rise and fall of great men, both biblical and historical. Shakespeare's *Richard III* is itself listed as a history in the First Folio. History as a specific dramatic genre did not exist as something exclusive, and one of Renaissance drama's true innovations was the split from the medieval sense of tragedy to include tragic stories based on revenge or personal desire. The history plays, however, are not part of this innovation, focusing instead on repetitive cycles of usurpation, violence, and civil unrest as God's will is either thwarted (Bolingbroke, Richard of York) or enacted (King Henry V). Even more vexingly, the history plays do not simply retell past events, but, similar to the Catholic mass (drama's origin, as it were), allows the audience to relive history in the way they would through the mystery and saints' plays.[2]

The generic blurriness of Shakespeare's history plays offers an excellent opportunity to explore the dramatic metamorphosis from a Catholic popular theater to a professional one. Playwrights and audiences alike shared a historical dramatic context that, like other popular practices, was firmly rooted in a medieval Catholic England trying to readjust itself to Reformation practices and beliefs,[3] which seemed unclear to most of the population as new terms, names, and services attempted to replace what was once

---

[1] Helen Cooper, *Shakespeare and the Medieval World*, Arden Shakespeare (London: 2010), 2.

[2] John Wasson, "The Morality Play: Ancestor of Elizabethan Drama?" *Comparative Drama* (1979): 210–21, accessed November 28, 2014, www.jstor.org.proxy-remote.galib.uga.edu/stable/41152838.

[3] Tamara Atkins, *The Drama of Reform: Theology and Theatricality, 1461–1553* (Turnhout, Belgium: Brepols, 2013).

unquestioned.[4] While it has become commonplace to link the histories with medieval morality plays,[5] scholars have also started to examine links between Shakespeare's history plays and other medieval dramatic forms, including the saints' plays.[6] The difficulty in this lies in the fact that there are no extant manuscripts of the Thomas Beckett plays, arguably among the most popular saints' plays in medieval and pre-reformation Tudor England. With their geographic and historical scope, the Thomas Beckett plays, focusing on English history, kings, and statecraft, are undoubtedly similar to the first tetralogy and the Henriad.[7]

While most current scholarship continues to focus on how early modern dramatists updated or reestablished the "rules" of historical drama, I will instead show, by examining other texts contemporary to or immediately predating Shakespeare and his audience's lives, how audiences' memory and recognition of previous hagiographic models necessarily inform *Richard III*. Philip Schwyzer demonstrates the necessity of shared cultural memory in creating the relationship between Richard and the Reformation. Even though Richard's reign and the Reformation are separated by almost 100 years, popular memory provides the link between Catholic medieval traditions[8] and the more recent "Reformation controversies [which] can be detected in Richard's apparent war against memory, his determination to cut the ties between the present and the past so that the future may be his."[9] The longevity of popular memory is the lynchpin in understanding what *Richard III* meant to its audiences. Because morality plays and saints' plays were being performed or revived within sixty years or so of the premiere of *Richard III*, it is likely that its Renaissance audiences could recognize certain characters like Richard or Richmond as well as their spiritual and political significance.

---

[4] Eamon Duffy, Introduction to *The Stripping of the Altars: Traditional Religion in England, c.1400–c.1580*, 2nd ed. (New Haven, CT: Yale University Press, 2005).

[5] For more information see Wasson, 210–21.

[6] Alan C. Dessen, *Shakespeare and the Late Moral Plays* (Lincoln: University of Nebraska Press, 1986).

[7] Wasson, 210–21.

[8] Philip Schwyzer, "Lees and Moonshine: Remembering Richard III, 1485–1635," *Renaissance Quarterly* (2010): 876.

[9] Ibid., 877.

While less recognizable to our eyes, Shakespeare's audiences, many of whom were intimately familiar with religious drama and saints' plays,[10] would have noticed *Richard III*'s hagiographic tropes, themes, and allegories, as well as recognized the narrative arc and structure as that of a saint's story. Comparing *Richard III* to the medieval romance *Sir Gowther* and the Anglo-centric Thomas Becket legend will help illustrate how Shakespeare adapted and inverted the available hagiographic tropes to create his anti-saint play through plot and character parallels, moral binaries, and spiritual parody.

A saint must first be introduced and "proven" to the audience; as such, the opening lines of Caxton's "Life of S. Thomas" identifies Becket as "S. Thomas the martyr," the "son to Gilbert Beckett, a burgess of the city of London . . . born in the place where as now standeth the church called S. Thomas of Acre," who "was . . . profound in humility . . . in word and in ensample, and hewn and trenched in his passion."[11] Caxton's edition begins with a description of Becket's holiness and martyrdom while fixing him firmly within England's geography and history, a profound and distinctly English saint whose death was the direct result of an English, not biblical king, and a part of their own shared history.

Shakespeare follows suit in Richard's identification as a force of evil in *Henry VI*, part 3, when Henry VI, moments before Richard murders him, declares:

> The owl shriek'd at thy birth, an evil sign;
> The night-owl cried, aboding luckless time;
> Dogs howl'd, and hideous tempest shook down trees;
> . . .
> an indigested and deformed lump,
> . . .
> Teeth hadst thou in thy head when thou wast born,
> To signify thou cam'st to bite the world.[12]

---

[10] Duffy, "Introduction."

[11] William Caxton, *Legenda Aurea*, "The Life of S. Thomas of Canterbury [Thomas Becket]" (London, 1483), Fordham University Web site, accessed February 20, 2015, https://legacy.fordham.edu/halsall/basis/goldenlegend/GoldenLegend-Volume1.asp.

[12] William Shakespeare, *The Third Part of Henry the Sixth*, in *The Riverside Shakespeare* (Boston: Houghton Mifflin, 1974), 671–707.

Henry's lengthy description is for the audience only; like Becket, Richard's role in the War of the Roses was already known. Henry and Richard's exchange is less about edification and more about identification; by using the same narrative structure as Caxton's "Life of S. Thomas," Richard's morality and place in English history has been established and, with his subsequent regicide, proved. Throughout the entirety of Caxton's and Shakespeare's texts, Becket's and Richard's moral identification is repeatedly confirmed: Becket is never referred to as anything less than "S. Thomas," while Richard, in both Henry VI, part 3, and Richard III, is consistently aligned with negative animal imagery ("elvish-marked, abortive, rooting hog," "a cockatrice," "thou toad") or demonic imagery ("the son of Hell" and "hell's black intelligencer").[13] Just as we never doubt that the Golden Legend's Becket is anything but good, the audience is never allowed to forget that Richard is anything but evil.

Although Shakespeare's representation of Richard's life in Henry VI, part 3, and Richard III intersects with the "Life of S. Thomas," both as presented in the Golden Legend and as it was played in the myriad non-extant Thomas Becket plays, his character is also indebted to Sir Gowther's eponymous hero, an unapologetically violent, distinctly un-Christian knight who, through extreme penance, finds God and forgiveness. Gowther's characterization as a reformed anti-saint, whose story embodies the good-versus-evil structural binary at play within hagiography, served as a model for the evil, disfigured Richard featured in Shakespeare's source material, notably Thomas More's vernacular The History of King Richard III and Bernard Andres's congratulatory Tudor history, Historia Henrici Septimi. Miracle and morality plays, as well as romances and romantic hagiographies, typically feature figures recognizable by their demonic likeness, made obvious by misshapen physiques, lying, extreme violence, aggression, and, more often than not, a crafty, cunning charm and charisma.

Sir Gowther is literally a "bad seed"; his duchess mother, threatened with divorce unless she conceives, retreats outside to pray for help, whereupon a man appears, seemingly her husband, with whom

---

[13] Shakespeare, Richard III, 1.3 line 697, 4.1 line 2532, 4.3 line 2919, 1.3 line 699, 4.3 line 2842.

she copulates. Her "husband" then informs her he is one of Hell's minions in disguise, and has impregnated her. As demon-spawn go, Gowther does not disappoint: born with teeth and a taste for blood, he manages to kill nine nurses before the age of one.[14] The local knights, who were rapidly losing their spouses to Gowther's infant jaws, refused to offer their wives' wet-nursing services any longer, forcing the duchess to nurse him herself, with terrifying results:

> He snaffulld to hit soo
> He rofe tho hed fro tho brest–
> Scho fell backeward and cald a prest,
> To chambur fled hym froo.[15]

Unsurprisingly, Gowther grows into a wild, violent young man, and his demonic tendencies are reflected in his weapon: the savage falchion.[16] A falchion is a short single-bladed sword, similar to a machete, whose truncated length and wide tip make it an excellent weapon for activities like cleaving—it combines the brutality of a club with the cutting power of a sword. Interestingly, Richard is also aligned with the falchion, as Anne remarks during Edward's funeral procession that his "bloody falchion smokes in [Edward's] blood."[17] Gowther's evilness and hellish lineage culminates in the rape and murder-by-fire of an entire convent, shortly after which he finds out his father was not human, but one of Hell's number. For once Gowther is shamed, and decides to atone for his birth and sin by making a pilgrimage to Rome, where, after being set a penance of silence, he is reformed.

Like Gowther, Shakespeare's Richard is a prodigious child born with teeth (and all they entail). Richard's mother, like Sir Gowther's duchess, feels she has birthed something monstrous, "A cockatrice . . . hatched to the world / Whose unavoided eye is murderous"[18] a child who, in an echo of Gowther's youth and early adulthood,

---

[14] Anonymous, *Sir Gowther*, ed. Anne Laskaya and Eve Salisbury, lines 118–20, accessed March 5, 2015, http://d.lib.rochester.edu/teams/text/laskaya-and-salisbury-middle-english-breton-lays-sir-gowther-introduction.

[15] Anonymous, lines 129–32.

[16] Anonymous, line 142.

[17] Shakespeare, *Richard III*, 1.2, line 190.

[18] Ibid., 4.1, lines 2534–35.

cam'st on earth to make the earth my hell;
A grievous burden was thy birth to me,
Tetchy and wayward was thy infancy,
Thy school-days frightful, desperate, wild and furious,
Thy prime of manhood daring, bold and venturous,
Thy age confirmed, proud, subtle, bloody, treacherous.[19]

The Duchess of York's only remaining son, Richard is his mother's disfigurement, a public declaration of his unnaturalness, which, coupled with the excessive animal imagery, hints at his potential demonic status. Unlike Gowther, whose eventual redemption allows him to participate in both the saint and anti-saint traditions, Richard, incapable of seeking forgiveness, is called to the life of an anti-saint.

Prayer and invocation, such powerful tools in Becket's hands, are inverted and parodied in *Richard III*. King Richard's use of parodic prayer (swords instead of rosaries), is, perhaps, the strongest link between Becket and Richard as opposite sides of the same hagiographic coin. Saint Thomas is martyred while celebrating Mass: "on Christmas day S. Thomas made a sermon at Canterbury in his own church, and weeping, prayed the people to pray for him, for he knew well his time was nigh, and there executed the sentence on them that were against the right of holy church."[20] Richard, on the other hand, wonders why he and his forces should waste time "numb'ring our Ave-Maries with our beads," recommending instead: "Shall we on the helmets of our foes / Tell our devotion with revengeful arms."[21] Becket's piety, which was capable of changing capon into fish, is answered by Richard's knowing parody of the pious:

But then I sigh, and with a piece of scripture
Tell them that God bids us do good for evil,
And thus I clothe my naked villainy
With old odd ends stolen out of holy writ,
And seem a saint when most I play the devil.[22]

---

[19] Ibid., 4.4, lines 2943–48.

[20] Caxton, "The Life of S. Thomas of Canterbury [Thomas Becket]."

[21] Shakespeare, *The Third Part of Henry the Sixth*, 2.1 lines 162–64.

[22] Shakespeare, *Richard III*, 1.3 lines 810–14.

Becket's martyrdom and sainthood were almost immediately acknowledged by others, including his murderers who

> found in a chest two shirts of hair made full of great knots, and then they said: Certainly he was a good man; and coming down into the churchward they began to dread and fear that the ground would not have borne them, and were marvellously aghast, but they supposed that the earth would have swallowed them all quick. And then they knew that they had done amiss.[23]

Richard, likewise, quickly "canonizes" himself as an anti-saint, with the audience's approbation:

> I am determined to prove a villain
> And hate the idle pleasures of these days.
> Plots have I laid, inductions, dangerous,
> By drunken prophesies, libels and dreams
> . . .
> I am subtle, false and treacherous.[24]

And, while Saint Thomas privately suffered daily penance in service of Christ, Richard openly and mockingly alludes to himself as a grotesque Christ:

> I'll make my heaven to dream upon the crown,
> And whiles I live, t' account this world but hell,
> Until my misshap'd trunk that bears this head
> Be round impaled with a glorious crown.
> . . .
> And I—like one lost in a thorny wood,
> That rents the thorns, and is rent with the thorns.[25]

His claim, a perversion of Christ's passion, is public and self-proclaimed. He is identified with his moral bearing in the same manner as Becket, but in a distinctly unholy way—he enjoys his role and position too much, glories in the grotesquery of his faith, to be anything other than the unholy version of the sanctified.

---

[23] Caxton, "The Life of S. Thomas of Canterbury [Thomas Becket]."
[24] Shakespeare, *Richard III*, 1.1 lines 32–39.
[25] Shakespeare, *The Third Part of Henry the Sixth*, 3.2 lines 165–72.

Richard's parodic inversion of prayer and Catholic imagery is further enhanced by his confessorial relationship with the audience to whom he is shriven. Instead of searching for forgiveness and redemption, however, he revels in their approval. In stark contrast with Saint Thomas, who "fell down on his knees and said, full sore weeping: O good Lord, I acknowledge that I have offended, and for mine offence and trespass this trouble cometh to holy church, I purpose, good Lord, to go to Rome for to be assoiled of mine offences,"[26] Richard participates in a conspiratorial, not penitential, relationship with his confessors:

> I am a villain—yet I lie, I am not.
> . . .
> My conscience hath a thousand several tongues,
> And every tongue brings in a several tale,
> And every tale condemns me for a villain.
> Perjury, perjury in the highest degree,
> Murder, stern murder, in the direst degree.
> All several sins, all used in each degree
> Throng to the bar, crying all, "Guilty, guilty!"[27]

Like a confession, he notes his sins (murder and lying), as well as his guilt, which is not only implied through his act of confession but clearly stated in his monologue. Instead of Becket's prayer and pilgrimage—his self-imposed penance in preparation for the martyrdom he knows is coming—Richard, who is not looking to calm his spirit, proceeds on his own distorted pilgrimage as he goes into his final battle, where he, like Becket, knows his doom awaits: "let us to it pell mell, / If not to heaven, then hand in hand to hell!"[28]

Shakespeare's adaptive inversion of hagiography's generic standards allowed him to create his alternately vibrant and chilling portrait of Richard. His anti-hagiography is not some sort of pick-and-mix; he did not shop Sir Gowther for characteristics A and B, or select setting C and theme D from Thomas Becket. Rather, Sir Gowther and Caxton's Life of Thomas Becket represent hagiography's dramatic and textual cultural currency as a tradition uniquely

---

[26] Caxton, "The Life of S. Thomas of Canterbury [Thomas Becket]."

[27] Shakespeare, Richard III, 5.3 lines 3653–61.

[28] Shakespeare, Richard III, 5.3 lines 3782–83.

capable of presenting Richard's innate immorality with the same detail previously devoted to saints' lives. Interestingly, the urge to discuss Richard III in hagiographic terms has not lessened, especially with the discovery of his body; more than 500 years after his death, the question of a moral or immoral Richard remains as salient as ever. The Richard III Society, among others, is leading the way to "cleanse" Shakespeare's anti-saint. Like Chaucer's pilgrims on the way to Thomas Becket's shrine, some Richard III scholars and enthusiasts have established pilgrimage routes and stops related to Richard's life, reign, and death. Volunteers continue to contribute and pay for Richard III statues, commemorative Yorkist altar cloths and banners, and the establishment of official Ricardian historic sites, all reminiscent of pre-canonization saints' cults, which were created by local communities rather than official religious institutions. The literary Richard, the anti-saint, is being inverted once more.

Hagiography was not a form relegated to the medieval past, but a genre that remained popular and largely unchanged until the seventeenth century and, at least in the case of Richard, is still active today. Early Tudors' and Shakespeare's Richards, as well as the contemporary Richard III Society's depiction of him, have made no discernible changes to hagiographic conventions. The literary Richard is not, and has never been, historically verifiable, which is neither hagiography's intent nor purpose. Like saint's legends, Richard's life is a conflation of the amazing and the factual, just as Shakespeare's *Richard III* is more than just a history or piece of Tudor myth; instead, *Richard III* provides an example of Renaissance hagiography, a Protestant adaptation of that most Catholic and medieval of literary traditions.

University of Georgia

Deny, Omit, and Disavow:
Becoming Ben Jonson

Melissa Geil

T HE information we have on the actual play *The Isle of Dogs* provides a picture of the play's writing, performance, and reception. In August of 1597, "Uppon informacion given us of a lewd plaie . . . contanynge very seditious and sclanderous matter, wee caused some of the players to be apprehended and comytted to pryson, one of them was not only an actor but a maker of the said plaie."[1] Ben Jonson, Gabriel Spenser, and Robert Shaa were put in prison, accused of sedition mongering, while John Marston and Thomas Nashe fled London. While in prison, Jonson— the "maker"—was questioned in order to assess two things: where Nashe, Marston, and the other actors were, and the location and number of copies of the play. And even though the judges "plac'd two damn'd Villains to catch advantage" with Jonson, "he was advertised by his keeper" of the situation and kept silent, only responding with yes or no.[2]

In the aftermath of this episode, both Nashe and Jonson actively distanced themselves from the play. Nashe writes of the play in *Lenten Stuffe*: "An imperfect embryon I may well call it, for having begun but the induction and the first act of it, the other four acts without my consent, or the least guess of my drift or scope, by the players were supplied, which bred both their trouble and mine,

---

[1] *Acts of the Privy Council of England*, New Series, ed. John Roche Dasent, 27 vols. (London: H. M. Stationary Office, 1903), 27:338.

[2] "Conversations with Drummond" (256–60), quoted in *Ben Jonson*, ed. C. H. Herford and Percy Simpson, 11 vols. (Oxford: Clarendon Press, 1925–63), 11:574.

too."[3] Nashe's disavowal is twofold: he insists that the majority of the play was not written by him, and he claims to have no prior knowledge of the inclusion of seditious material in the text. He blames it all on the actors.

While Jonson did not deny his involvement as vehemently as Nashe, he certainly did not admit his association with the play while in prison, and he and the other actors were eventually released. He does, however, call upon this episode of imprisonment in another time of need, when, in 1605, Jonson is imprisoned again for *Eastward Ho!* In his letter to Robert Cecil, Jonson defends his evolution as an author, "since my first error, which yet is punished in me more with my shame than it was with my bondage—I have so attempered my style that I have given no cause to any man of grief; and if to any ill, by touching at any general vice, it hath always been with a regard, and sparing of particular persons." In calling *The Isle of Dogs* his "first error," Jonson actively distances himself from his earlier writings, claiming the experience as something akin to a lesson learned, a careful retroactive edit of his view of an earlier work.

This edit is very much a part of the way in which Jonson should be considered as an author. His deliberate and painstaking work constructing his authorial representation is most obvious in his presentation of the 1616 *Workes*. But when we consider Jonson's authorial identity, the case of *The Isle of Dogs* suggests compelling evidence that authorship is as much about what one leaves out as it is about the writing to which one lays claim. Consider the rest of Jonson's letter to Cecil:

> I beseech your most honorable lordship, suffer not other men's errors or faults past to be my crimes, but let me be examined, both by all my works past and this present, and not trust to rumour but my books (for she is an unjust deliverer both of great and small actions) whether I have ever, in anything I have written, private or public, given offence to a nation, to any public order or state, or any person of honour or authority, but have equally laboured to keep their dignity as mine own person, safe.[4]

---

[3] Thomas Nashe, *Lenten Stuffe*, in *The Works of Thomas Nashe*, ed. R. B. McKerrow, 5 vols. (Oxford: Blackwell, 1966), 3.153–54.

[4] Ben Jonson, "Letter 3, to Robert Cecil, first Earl of Salisbury" in *The Cambridge Edition of the Works of Ben Jonson*, eds. David Bevington,

Jonson asks to be examined by his works past and present. What must be considered in this request, however, is that several of Jonson's earlier works, including *The Isle of Dogs*, had been destroyed or were "lost." All that is left of them is "rumour." More specifically, Jonson asks to be examined by "my books"; a significant request given Jonson's insistence on involvement in the printing of many of his plays and masques. Thus, much of what we know about Jonson's work as author necessarily involves the deliberate and purposeful omission, disavowal, and editing of his work.

In his biography of Jonson, Ian Donaldson writes: "The number of Jonson's works that do not survive is considerably larger than is often supposed. Of the numerous plays that he wrote, in particular, at the outset of his career, most are known only by name, or through some general reference. Jonson was a discriminating writer, who did not attempt to preserve everything he wrote."[5]

Michel Foucault's consideration of the "author function" establishes authorship as a juridical category emerging in literary cultures defined, at least in part, by surveillance and censorship. While Jonson omitted, dismissed, or revised some of his work to avoid prison,[6] the "author function" does not consistently work as a model, thus offering an incomplete picture of Jonson. Joseph Loewenstein argues that profit, not censorship, drives the evolving concept of authorship. Authorship is fundamentally possessive, according to Loewenstein, and the lengths to which Jonson goes to acquire rights to his works demonstrates his role in the emerging connection between authors and their intellectual property rights in the early modern period.[7] But then how do we account for moments where Jonson's model of authorship appears more dispossessive than possessive?

The emergence of the figure of the "author," in the case of Jonson in particular, works as an ideological fantasy, in the sense that it requires a "misrecognition of a social reality which is a part

---

Martin Butler, and Ian Donaldson, 7 vols. (Cambridge, UK: Cambridge Univ. Press, 2012), 2:646–47.

[5] Ian Donaldson, *Ben Jonson: A Life* (Oxford Univ. Press, 2011), 124.

[6] See Joseph Loewenstein on *Sejanus* in *Ben Jonson and Possessive Authorship* (Cambridge, UK: Cambridge Univ. Press, 2002), 150–51.

[7] Ibid., 151.

of this reality itself," in the terms of Slavoj Žižek.[8] In the case of works that Jonson dismissed, omitted, or heavily edited, ideology functions as fetishistic disavowal, where, despite understanding that one's actions are, to some degree, futile or will produce a negative outcome, one will do it anyway: "they know very well what they are doing, but still, they are doing it."[9] As Neal Magee argues, when Žižek uses the term disavowal, he denotes "consciously setting aside knowledge or holding two contradictory positions at the same time . . . As an expression of desire, fetishistic disavowal functions to sustain what he calls 'ideological fantasy,' a positive means of structuring and framing experience."[10] One way to consider Jonson's omissions, denials, and disavowals may be to think about them in terms of the "ideological fantasy" of authorship, what it means to produce a body of work conscientiously meant to live on in one's stead. In this fantasy, authorship is both possessive and dispossessive; it requires an ideological card trick whereby only the works he elects to edit and attentively shepherd into print represent Jonson as an author. Just as in the letter Jonson writes to Cecil quoted earlier, if errors were made, they were "other men's," and if the work is not included in the 1616 *Workes*, it may as well not exist: "not trust to rumour, but my books."

Jonson, more than any other author of his time fastidiously edited and shepherded his work into print. The works he leaves behind—*The Isle of Dogs*, *Eastward Ho!*, and *The Case Is Altered*—and the works he chooses to give his attention to, such as *Sejanus*, allow for a consideration of Ben Jonson's authorship that suggests the value and implications of distancing one's self from works deemed unsuitable for preservation. Moreover, they demonstrate how Jonson's authorial identity can be understood as an ideological fantasy that requires disavowal to function.

---

[8] Slavoj Žižek, *The Sublime Object of Ideology* (London: Verso, 2008), 25.

[9] Žižek, 25.

[10] Neal Magee, "Remembering to Forget: Theological Tropologies of Confession and Disavowal" (PhD diss., Syracuse University, 2004), abstract.

Left Out: *The Case Is Altered*

In the 1616 folio, the first work that appears is *Every Man in His Humor*. This was not, however, the first single-authored play by Jonson. That distinction belongs to *The Case Is Altered*, written in May or June of 1597 (the same year as *The Isle of Dogs*). And while the quarto text of *Every Man in His Humor* suggests "a manuscript adjusted for print," as Joseph Loewenstein contends, *The Case Is Altered* enjoyed no such attention.[11] Moreover, according to Loewenstein, Jonson also placed his mark on the print editions of *Every Man in His Humor*, *Cynthia's Revels*, *Poetaster*, and *Sejanus*, among others, making *The Case Is Altered* a standout for Jonson's lack of involvement.[12]

When *The Case Is Altered* was entered into the Stationers Register in 1609—twelve years after its initial performance—no author was listed. The quarto print history is somewhat puzzling. In the initial printing, Jonson is listed as the author, but in a second printing, his name is omitted, most likely the result of a printer error, as the copy was corrected for most of the run.[13] Given that Jonson had some hand in the printing of most of his plays written in the period after 1600, it suggests that his lack of involvement may have been deliberate.

According to Bob Miola, "Jonson appears to have had nothing to do with the printing of *The Case Is Altered*. The quarto lacks any sign of his presence—title-page claims, Latin motto, dedication, commendatory verses, epistle dedicatory, preface, acrostic argument, prologue, and epilogue."[14] Donaldson similarly claims "*The Case Is Altered* survives despite Jonson's own wishes, for he made no known attempt in in later years to claim it as his own."[15]

A number of theories have been offered to explain both Jonson's missing contributions to the initial printing of *The Case Is Altered* and the play's absence from the 1616 folio. Herford and Simpson

---

[11] Loewenstein, *Ben Jonson and Possessive Authorship*, 142–44.

[12] Ibid., 142.

[13] Bob Miola, "*The Case Is Altered*: Textual Essay," in *The Cambridge Edition of the Works of Ben Jonson Online*, 3.

[14] Ibid., 3.

[15] Donaldson, 109.

make a case for the play as "a rare example of a Jonson text which
may be described as thoroughly bad,"[16] suggesting that Jonson's distancing himself from the work had primarily to do with the fact that
it was simply not up to par with his later material. Even then, however, Jonson revised much of the material from the play in advance
of its appearance in both the quarto and the folio.[17] The Cambridge
editors claim that "[c]ritics have largely agreed that Jonson dis-
owned the earlier work," but they counter that these critics rely on
"unproven (unprovable) assumptions about the author's intentions
and construction of his career."[18] Instead, they suggest that copyright laws may have been an issue for the inclusion of the play in
the folio. J. M. Nosworthy suggests that *The Case Is Altered* may not
have been included in the folio because of a collaborator issue, pos-
iting Henry Porter as Jonson's writing partner.[19] Nosworthy claims
that "it was doubtless his purpose to preserve nothing that was not
entirely his own, and though it was arrogant there was honesty in its
fulfillment."[20] Finally, Loewenstein offers a detailed account of the
copyright history of play that affirms the play's status as an anomaly
in terms of Jonson's lack of involvement.[21]

---

[16] Herford and Simpson, 3.96.

[17] David L. Gants and Tom Lockwood, "The Printing and Publishing of Ben Jonson's Works" in *The Cambridge Ben Jonson*. 5 vols. 1:clxxi.
David Kay disputes this claim that *The Case Is Altered* was unsuccessful in
his "The Shaping of Ben Jonson's Career: A Reexamination of Facts and
Problems," *Modern Philology* (1970): 224–37.

[18] "Introduction to *The Case is Altered*," in *The Cambridge Ben Jonson*, 1.5.

[19] J. M. Nosworthy, "The Case Is Altered," *The Journal of English and
Germanic Philology* 51, no. 1 (January 1952): 61–70. Nosworthy also claims
that the play is an altered version of another "lost" Jonson play, *Hot Anger
Cold Too Soon*.

[20] Ibid., 70. The Cambridge Editors also offer this line of argument,
stating "Jonson may simply have excluded *The Case is Altered* from his
Works because it was not solely his" (1:6).

[21] Loewenstein writes that "The poor quality of the text of this long-
unpublished play and the absence of the usual signs of Jonsons's involvement
in text preparation *may* suggest some sort of irregularity in the acquisition
of copy . . . It is thus difficult to dispel the impression of irregularity: either
Stansby (or Burre or the folio syndicate) failed to come to an accommo-
dation with whomever held the copyright, or Jonson repudiated the play

The theories set forth so far for the play's absence from the folio promote the following reasons for omission: collaborator issues, bad writing, and copyright problems. It is noteworthy that a number of other "lost plays" are from this early period, including *The Isle of Dogs*, *Hot Anger Cold to Soon*, *The Page of Plymouth*, and *Robert II, King of Scots*, though these are all thought to be collaborative works. The standout play from Jonson's early career is *Every Man in His Humor*, which, according to John Aubrey, was Jonson's first success: Jonson "having suffered previous failures at the Curtain,' undertook again to write a play and hit it admirably well, viz. *Every man . . .* which was his first good one."[22] The argument that *The Case Is Altered* was not a commercial success could be made here as a reason for lack of involvement in the printing. That the play may well have been a collaborative effort could have stifled its publication, since, of Jonson's early collaborative plays, only *Eastward Ho!* was published (1605), and then without Jonson's input. There is also the possibility that Jonson's play, as the property of Pembroke's Men, was not his to help shepherd through the publication process. Regardless, *The Case Is Altered*, as a result of its lack of inclusion in the folio and Jonson's lack of involvement in the printing of the play, is a prime example of authorial disavowal by omission. As such, it allows for us to think critically about Jonson's early career in terms of quality of work, experience with collaboration, and establishment of his authorial legacy through elision.

The Trouble with Collaborators:
Eastward Ho! and *Sejanus*

As stated earlier, *Eastward Ho!* is another work notable for Jonson's lack of involvement in the printing of the quarto and for its

---

on aesthetic grounds—or Jonson repudiated the play because of persistent annoyance over the original circumstances of its publication. It may be observed, however, that the Folio does include a version of *Queenes* although no record is preserved of how the rights of copy were secured, a circumstance that is, in itself, unusual." *Ben Jonson and Possessive Authorship*, 192–93n121.

[22] John Aubrey, *Brief Lives, Chiefly of Contemporaries*, quoted in *Cambridge Ben Jonson*, 1.113.

absence in the 1616 *Workes*. Multiple explanations have been offered for these absences. Jonson was in prison shortly before or after the initial publication of the play in 1605 for the play's anti-Scottish satire, and all of the quarto versions from 1605 lack what would appear to be authorial modifications that would indicate his involvement.[23] The Cambridge editors (Gossett and Kay) offer numerous theories regarding how such a controversial play was printed at all, ranging from the printer's cashing in on the controversy by rushing the print process to the printing of the play actually causing the imprisonment of Jonson, Chapman, and Marston.[24] Loewenstein presumes its absence from the folio due to its collaborative authorship,[25] and Gregory Chaplin suggests that *Eastward Ho!* soured Jonson on collaboration forever, stating that *Eastward Ho!* supported a "familiar pattern of collaboration, provocation, and punishment established by *The Isle of Dogs* and *Sejanus*, a pattern linking collaboration and excess that Jonson could not have failed to notice . . . It was the last play on which he collaborated."[26]

Regardless of whether or not *Eastward Ho!* convinced Jonson not to collaborate on plays from then on, it did not prevent Jonson from adapting another play on which he collaborated, *Sejanus*, for publication. But in shepherding his play to publication in 1605, Jonson ensured the play was a single-authored endeavor, informing the reader that "this book . . . is not the same with that which was acted on the public stage, wherein a second pen had good share; in place of which I have rather chosen to put weaker (and no doubt less pleasing) of mine own, than to defraud so happy a genius of his right by my loathed usurpation."[27]

Sejanus is a compelling case to consider for both Jonson's involvement in the quarto and folio editions because it problematizes the

---

[23] Suzanne Gossett, "*Eastward Ho!:* Textual Essay." *The Cambridge Edition of the Works of Ben Jonson Online.*

[24] "Introduction" to *Eastward Ho! Cambridge Edition of the Works of Ben Jonson* 2:533–34.

[25] Loewenstein, *Ben Jonson and Possessive Authorship*, 188.

[26] Gregory Chaplin, "'Divided Amongst Themselves': Collaboration and Anxiety in Jonson's *Volpone*." *ELH* 69, no. 1 (Spring 2002): 65. Chaplin, of course, is not considering Jonson's masques here.

[27] *Cambridge Edition of the Works of Ben Jonson*, 2:215.

theories that Jonson did not publish collaborative work, or that Jonson opted not to print works that got him in trouble with the law. Moreover, *Sejanus*, like *The Case Is Altered*, was not considered a success in the theater. In the quarto printing, Jonson's dedication suggests the play's calamitous reception:

> If ever any ruin were so great as to survive, I think this be one I send you: *The Fall of Sejanus*. It is a poem that, if I well remember, in your Lordship's sight suffered no less violence from our people here than the subject of it did from the rage of the people of Rome; but with a different fate, as (I hope) merit: for this hath outlived their malice, and begot itself a greater favour than he lost.[28]

Sejanus, viewed with "malice" by the audience, and containing lines that could land him in prison—he was summoned before the Privy Council for the play—receives a second life in print. The extensive prefatory material in the quarto edition indicates a keen attention to the text's appearance, and demonstrates Jonson's efforts to secure a favorable reception for the play in publication. Even though the play could have been excluded from the folio based on the criteria that critics have argued as reasons for his elision of *The Case Is Altered* and *Eastward Ho!*, Jonson actively and doggedly lays claim to the text. In the paratextual material, he attests to his unassisted authorship, and guides interpretation, a shining example of Loewenstein's "possessive" author.

But the possessive authorship of *Sejanus* is, in itself, an example of the author as a kind of ideological fantasy. The *Sejanus* Jonson creates in the Quarto version, lives anew as a completely different entity. No longer the subject of audience indifference or virulence, Jonson fashions both a text and a reader for his work, acknowledging that the previous version exists, while replacing the play and the audience with a single-authored fantasy where the reader is an "Understander."[29]

Jonson, like Nashe, was aware of the potential advantages and pitfalls of printed works, but his approach to negotiating his status as

---

[28] Ibid., 2:212.

[29] Ben Jonson, "To the Reader" from *The Alchemist* (1610), *The Cambridge Edition of the Works of Ben Jonson Online*.

an author demonstrates the reasons why modern critics have often cited Jonson as the first example of an author as we now understand the term. Sara van den Berg heralds Jonson as "the first English writer to exploit the humanist concept of authorship by publishing his own collected works in folio."[30] David Riggs ties Jonson's establishment of his literary identity to "the emergence of authorship as a full-time vocation."[31] Joseph Loewenstein's works are concerned with, among other concepts of contract and authorship, the formation of Jonson's literary authority.[32] And, while these claims have certainly not gone unchallenged, even those who posit alternative theories of the development of early modern authorship must contend with the figure of Ben Jonson, whose literary presence stands as something of a "Herculean figure, single-handedly transforming the concept and the status of the author."[33]

This picture of early modern authorship remains incomplete without a reckoning of Jonson's dispossessive or partial authorship. Printed authorship in the early modern period, as Jonson fashioned it, required editing, curating, repudiation, and discarding.

In his prologue to the folio version of *Every Man in His Humor*, Jonson explains why he moved the location of the play to London, stating his play deals with:

> deeds, and language, such as men do use:
> And persons, such as comedie would chuse,
> When she would shew an Image of the times,
> And sport with humane follies, not with crimes.

---

[30] Sara van den Berg, "Ben Jonson and the Ideology of Authorship," in *Ben Jonson's 1616 Folio*, ed. Jennifer Brady and W. H. Herendeen (Newark: University of Delaware Press, 1991), 111.

[31] David Riggs, *Ben Jonson: A Life* (Cambridge, MA: Harvard Univ. Press, 1989), 3.

[32] See Joseph Loewenstein's *The Author's Due: Printing and the Prehistory of Copyright* (Chicago, IL: Univ. of Chicago Press, 2002) and *Ben Jonson and Possessive Authorship*.

[33] This quote comes from Charles Cathcart's recent article "Authorship, Indebtedness, and the Children of the King's Revels," *SEL* 45, no. 2 (2005): 366. Cathcart refutes this ideal version of Ben Jonson as author, rather arguing for a more diverse range of authors who demonstrate "powerful authorial agency," particularly John Marston.

Except, we make'hem such by loving still
Our popular errors, when we know th'are ill.
I meane such errors, as you'll all confesse
By laughing at them, they deserve no lesse:
Which when you heartily doe, there's hope left, then,
You, that have so grac'd monsters, may like men.[34]

Jonson refers to *The Isle of Dogs* as his "first error" in defending himself against accusations about *Eastward Ho!*, but in this prologue,
Jonson suggests that errors are something to be loved and laughed
at, something that reminds us that we are human. As an "author,"
however, Jonson's strategically cuts, omits, and denies involvement
in much of his early work (and some of his later works), suggesting that the "authorial Jonson" he cultivates in print seeks to excise
errors in favor of a desire to shape his legacy and memory.

Later in his career, Jonson discussed what it means for a story to
be "whole." In considering classic works by Homer, Virgil, Sophocles, and others, Jonson accounted for Sophocles's *Ajax* as a "whole"
story. Sophocles does not include every single thing that happened
in Ajax's life; rather, he puts together pieces of his life in order to
tell a story, "These things agree and hang together, not as they were
done, but as *seeming* to be done, which made the action whole, entire,
and absolute."[35] In shaping his authorial identity through a process
of possession and dispossession, ownership and omission, Jonson
created a seeming whole from parts. He included *Every Man in his
Humor*, but left out *The Case Is Altered*; he dropped *Eastward Ho!*
and fashioned *Sejanus* into a single authored and very different play.
He recast prior events as errors, and in asserting the primacy of his
printed books, attempted to create himself anew in print.

University of North Carolina, Chapel Hill

---

[34] Jonson, *The Workes of Benjamin Jonson, 1616* (facsimile) (London:
The Scolar Press, 1976), 5–6.

[35] Ben Jonson, *Discoveries* (1641), *The Cambridge Edition of the Works
of Ben Jonson Online* (emphasis mine).

"What strange parallax or optic skill": *Paradise Regained* and the Masque

William A. Coulter

Book 3 of *Paradise Regained* begins as follows:

> So spake the Son of God, and Satan stood
> A while as mute confounded what to say,
> What to reply, confuted and convinced
> Of his weak arguing, and fallacious drift;[1]

And there in a nutshell is the problem for the entire poem, dramatically speaking: there can be no tension when it is clear how easily divinity sees through every contrivance of the Adversary. The lukewarm response of many critics to Milton's poem is well known, provoked in part by this lack of authentic emotional confrontation, and also by the verse in which the matter of the poem is expressed, so much lower in voltage than that of *Paradise Lost*. Roy Flannagan, in his introduction to the brief epic, gives a convenient sample of adjectives which have been applied to it: plain, bald, unadorned, flat, colorless, dry, muted, bleak.[2] To be fair, though, we should recall that Samuel Johnson, thought by many to be relentlessly hostile to Milton, remarked of *Paradise Regained* that "it is in many parts elegant, and every-where instructive," and that "had this poem been written not

---

[1] All citations from *The Poems of John Milton*, ed. John Carey and Alastair Fowler (London: Longmans, Green, 1968). Hereafter cited parenthetically in text by book and line.

[2] *The Riverside Milton*, ed. Roy Flannagan (Boston: Houghton Mifflin, 1998), 713.

by Milton, but by some imitator, it would have claimed and received universal praise."[3]

As it happens, there was a category of literary expression that flourished in the seventeenth century and that was also entirely lacking in dramatic tension or forward motion, namely the Stuart court masque. From the first couple of masques on, as soon as the form established its identity, it was clear what the climax would be; and as masque designer Inigo Jones became more and more ingenious, it was equally clear that the pleasures of the masque would be mostly the pleasures of visual surprise, as sudden dissolves, scene changes, descending clouds, opening rocks, and heaving mountains astonished the spectators. If there was conflict in the masque, it was pro forma—the conflict of the antimasques, which became part of the spectacle early on and which existed solely to be effortlessly banished.

Milton's own attempt at the masque was, of course, noticeably different, in that it was not dependent on visual spectacle and included a fairly extensive philosophical discussion at its core. Nevertheless it is significant that he did try the form in the 1630s, the decade of the most extravagantly sycophantic spectacles; that he made no objection to having it published in 1637; and that he was at pains to include the work in the 1645 poems. Nor did the theatrical frame of reference cease to be relevant after the masque: *Paradise Lost* is a vast structure that contains a great many things, so it is not surprising that it has been investigated in light of the stage.[4] In this essay, I should like to turn the same spotlight on *Paradise Regained*, to see how certain passages grow more vivid as we read them thus.

It is important to acknowledge that there is one element of the poem that does function as something of a mystery, propelling us toward clarification, and that is the meaning of the promise that Jesus will "sit on David's throne" (1.240). In the line quoted, Jesus himself is musing on what this might signify; Satan likewise is intrigued by this expression, and it remains uncertain to what degree

---

[3] *The Lives of the Poets*, ed. John H. Middendorf (New Haven, CT: Yale Univ. Press, 2010), 21.200.

[4] John Demaray, *Milton's Theatrical Epic: the Invention and Design of Paradise Lost* (Cambridge, MA: Harvard Univ. Press, 1980).

the statement is metaphorical, and to what degree it might denote an actual event. This "throne," then, becomes the focus of Satan's various acts of temptation.

To tempt someone, a goal is required, and a mechanism: to gain a prize, one argues, describes, questions, shows a piece of the loot. In *Paradise Lost*, Satan's temptations (of his followers, in book 5, and of Eve, in book 9) are built on rhetoric and dialectic. By the time those parts of the poem are reached, we have already had ample demonstration of his skill as a speaker, so we are not surprised that his address to his angelic cohort turns around the subtle manipulation of terms such as "the name / Of king," "Knee-tribute," "bend / The supple knee," "imperial titles," and so on; likewise with Eve, Satan rapidly sets out an array of arguments that, in their number and with their specious subtlety, overwhelm Eve's critical powers. In these passages, all depends on the power of the word—the only exception is the dream that he places in Eve's mind (4.800), and even there we have to wait for her own words to have any idea of its actual contents.

If the "throne of David," whatever thing that may be, is the goal to be achieved, then the question for the tempter becomes one of mechanism. What association was more natural, in the mid-seventeenth century, than throne and masque?[5] The masques' affirmation of the Stuart ideal is accomplished largely through a series of magical images—painted scenes full of allegorical significance (especially the "frontispiece" or proscenium) and scenes representing particular vistas or places, which are clearly liable at any time to be transformed into other vistas or places. There are flattering speeches, too, of course, but "the illusion of power" (to borrow Stephen Orgel's title) was one that was communicated through the unified arts, not primarily through words. The throne, then, comes to be understood as the agent from which change and improvement originate—and

---

[5] Barbara Lewalski notes that the passion narrative would in some ways have been a more logical sequel to *Paradise Lost*, but that Milton's choice of the temptation in the desert allowed him to stay away from the Charles-as-Christ figure so memorably expressed in *Eikon Basilike*. If there are memories of masques in *Paradise Regained*, as I am suggesting, they sound the courtly note but without invoking the notion of martyrdom. *The Life of John Milton* (Oxford: Blackwell, 2000), 511.

it doesn't matter whether the scene begins with "a delicious place by nature and art, where, in a valley environed with hills afar off, was seated a prospect of curious arbours of various forms" or whether it begins with "old Arches, old Palaces, decayed walls, parts of Temples, Theatres, Basilica's, and Therme, with confused heaps of broken Columns, Bases, Coronices and Statues,"[6] because we understand that in every case things are only going to get better. The power of the dissolve, of the transformation, is always hovering. This means, incidentally, that the images themselves, though they remind us that Inigo Jones won his contest with Ben Jonson, are nevertheless at the mercy of a greater power even than that of their creator—a point memorably made by D. J. Gordon in his reading of *Love's Welcome at Bolsover*.[7]

To pursue this theme, we must make our way through *Paradise Regained*, allowing our memories of masque sights and sounds to be triggered by what we find. By the time the poem was published, the court masque was largely a memory,[8] but it is worth noting the recent work of Lauren Shohet, through which we see that although the masques were elitist events performed (usually) one time only and attended by a limited number of privileged spectators, in fact there was much more widespread interest in them, and more dissemination of their texts and descriptions, than was previously thought.[9] The approach I am suggesting is perhaps less rarified than it might seem at first glance.

Satan's first impressive appearance in the poem is before his followers in council, gathered now not in Pandemonium but "in mid air . . . Within thick clouds and dark tenfold involved, / A gloomy consistory;"—that is, gods arrayed in their serried ranks in the

---

[6] *Tempe Restored*, in *Court Masques*, ed. David Lindley (Oxford: World's Classics, 1995), 156; *Coelum Britannicum*, in *The Poems of Thomas Carew*, ed. Rhodes Dunlap (Oxford: Clarendon Press, 1957), 154.

[7] "Poet and Architect: The Intellectual Setting of the Quarrel between Ben Jonson and Inigo Jones," in *The Renaissance Imagination*, ed. Stephen Orgel (Berkeley: Univ. of California Press, 1975), 77–101.

[8] Inga-Stina Ewbank, "Masques and Pageants," in *17th Century Britain: the Cambridge Cultural History*, ed. Boris Ford (Cambridge, UK: Cambridge Univ. Press, 1992), 117.

[9] Shohet, *Reading Masques: The English Masque and Public Culture in the Seventeenth Century* (Oxford: Oxford Univ. Press, 2010).

heavens, a common sight in the Italian intermedii—in the famous 1589 staging of *La Pellegrina*, for example, and one that Inigo Jones translated into his masque designs in various ways.[10] Satan will return to this setting at 2.117.

His first appearance to Jesus, however, is as an unassuming Spenserian figure, "an aged man in rural weeds."[11] Looking for confirmation that Jesus is the "son of God," he asks for a demonstration miracle, and it becomes clear within thirty lines that Jesus knows who he is. Satan does not, as Bertie Wooster might say, put much topspin on this temptation; the only elaboration is his statement that they in this desert "live on tough roots and stubs, to thirst inured / More than the camel." Satan boasts of his friendship to men, displayed classically through "oracles, portents, and dreams," and Jesus responds by pointing out that the classics are a dead letter: "henceforth oracles are ceased." This first essay at temptation has a perfunctory quality; it is brief and almost entirely lacking in appeal to the senses.

The next instance follows from the first (it still has to do with hunger), but profits from careful preparation and greatly enhanced production values, an emphasis on sight, smell, taste. Although in the devilish council in the middle air, Satan enumerates "worth . . . honor, glory, and popular praise" as engines of temptation, he determines to continue to employ hunger.

> Then forthwith to him takes a chosen band

> Of spirits likest to himself in guile
> To be at hand, and at his beck appear,
> If cause were to unfold some active scene
> Of various persons each to know his part . . .
>   (2.236–40)

---

[10] Italian examples in Allardyce Nicoll, *Stuart Masques and the Renaissance Stage* (New York: Harcourt Brace, 1938), 95, 108; English examples in John Peacock, *The Stage Designs of Inigo Jones* (Cambridge, UK: Cambridge Univ. Press, 1995), 108, 275.

[11] It is fitting that a Spenserian note is sounded at this moment, as Jesus will be seen to have many affinities with Guyon. See Richard Jordan, *The Quiet Hero: Figures of Temperance in Spenser, Donne, Milton, and Joyce* (Washington, DC: Catholic Univ. Press, 1989), chapter 4.

These assistants then appear in a carefully arranged dramatic scene as "tall stripling youths rich-clad" and "Nymphs of Diana's train" accompanying the groaning board that Jesus suddenly sees where nothing was before. This return engagement, significantly, begins with Satan now not a humble rustic but "seemlier clad, / As one in city, or court, or palace bred" (Italics added). The description of the comestibles is enlivened with references to classical myth and to the world of the romance, but when Jesus refuses, "both table and provision vanished quite / With sound of harpies' wings . . ." John Carey notes that this temptation, contrasted with the first one, "might seem resplendently solid, but Milton's description of it is carefully remote, and its instantaneous disappearance (2.402–3) as well as the suspiciously supernatural setting . . . help to shift it, in the reader's mind, to the realm of mirage and illusion . . ."[12] It is perhaps surprising that Carey makes no reference here to the masques, for the preparation, appearance, and disappearance of this spectacle all partake of their characteristics; we can easily imagine some of Inigo's machines at work, and the richly realized appeal to the senses is palpable.[13]

According to Luke's gospel, the second temptation is that of the kingdoms of the world. This turns out to be the most extensive and substantial in *Paradise Regained*, occupying much of books 3 and 4. The viewing point is a mountain—that is, an elevated single point to which all lines of sight converge, as they did to the throne in the masquing hall, and from which sweeping vistas may be seen. Here Satan points out Assyria, Ninevah, Babylon, and Persepolis before turning to the Parthian empire and its conflict with the Scythian. There follows a lively depiction of units in battle, "the field all iron," reaching its climax in an allusion to such martial tales "as romances tell." This vista then in effect vanishes; at any rate, it is looked at no more, as Satan advises Jesus to ally himself with the Parthians

---

[12] *The Poems of John Milton*, ed. Carey and Fowler, 1074. Every student of the poem must be indebted to Carey's meticulous examination of style and rhetoric, 1070–77. I do think, however, that he overstates the "elusiveness" of Milton's imagery.

[13] It is usual to note also an echo of the banquet in *The Tempest*: see, e.g., *Riverside Milton*, ed. Flannagan, 748. Carey does mention this in his note to 2.402–3.

against the Romans, and promptly links vista and throne to make his argument:

> By him thou shalt regain, without him not,
> That which alone can truly reinstall thee
> In David's royal seat . . .
>
> (3.371–73)

In the next phase, Satan brings Jesus to the western side of the mountain, from which he may contemplate the sights of Italy: first comes the epic narrator's general description, the river and the seven hills, towers and temples, palaces, baths, aqueducts, triumphal arches; then Satan's fuller explication, naming the Capitol, the imperial palace, "pillars and roofs / Carved work, the hand of famed artificers / In cedar, marble, ivory or gold," the gates, proconsuls and lictors coming and going, legions, the Appian way, the distant outposts of Empire.[14] The Roman visual language was, of course, featured everywhere in the Stuart masques.[15] Where Satan had counseled Jesus in book 3 to ally himself with the Parthians, here he focuses on the literal seat—that is, the throne—of Roman power; then in such a degenerate state, Jesus, he says, might "expel this monster from his throne / Now made a sty, and in his place ascending / A victor people free from servile yoke!" We are not surprised that he mentions David's throne at once.

Jesus's language as he rejects this "grandeur and majestic show / Of luxury" takes on more coloration than usual, with mention of the feasting, the crystal and pearl, the embassies, the "hollow compliments"—in other words, all the stuff of courts. His language glances

---

[14] Carey notes that the Roman panorama, by contrast with the Parthian one, is "situated in almost painstakingly specific surroundings," but he goes on to show how Milton's language initially suggests but then backs away from visual particularity, "slides back into the muddled splendor . . ." *The Poems of John Milton*, ed. Carey and Fowler, 1075–76.

[15] John Peacock, in defending Inigo Jones from Roy Strong's charge of being a "relentless copyist," points out that he, like Isaac Oliver, was engaged in a project whereby "the whole gamut of continental mannerist styles is self-consciously represented." Peacock, *The Stage Designs of Inigo Jones*, 15. For a sample, see Harris, Orgel, and Strong, *The King's Arcadia: Inigo Jones and the Stuart Court* (London: Arts Council of Great Britain, 1973), 68–81.

back to Satan's banquet in book 2, but situates it now in the context of absolutist political power. And indeed, in this passage Jesus indulges in a bit of figurative language:

> Know therefore when my season comes to sit
> On David's throne, it shall be like a tree
> Spreading and overshadowing all the earth,
> Or as a stone that shall to pieces dash
> All monarchies besides throughout the world . . .
> (4.146–50)

Although this language comes from the books of Daniel and Isaiah, the effect is not unlike a dissolve or scene change: the sliding flats are drawn apart, the periaktoi turn, the Roman imagery disappears and is replaced by the deceptively simple, almost impresa-like, tree-throne.

According to Satan, he has now learned that Jesus is immune to temptations of "the kingdoms of the world," so he turns instead to the kingdom of the mind: "Be famous then / By wisdom." And so he adjusts the line of sight, nearer by south-west, to bring Greece into view. The description in this case is brief: walks and shades, the olive grove of Academe, flowery Hymettus, the stream Illissus; this is preparatory to an enumeration of teachers, poets, tragic playwrights, orators, and philosophers. Although this temptation is said to be different, it functions similarly to the Roman sequence: the scene comes first, then its interpretation, then we cease to note it as it fades away. This temptation is also rejected, and the rejection involves yet another denigration of the classics. Jesus again indulges in a bit of pictorial imagery when he observes that whoever "seeks in these / True wisdom, finds her not, or by delusion / Far worse, her false resemblance only meets, / An empty cloud." This has something of a light touch: Inigo's cloud machines were among his favorite playthings, and clouds routinely opened to reveal gods or masquers in all their finery; it is amusing to imagine one "empty."

The storm scene, when Satan has returned Jesus to the wilderness for the nonce, is perhaps more reminiscent of the playhouse than the masquing hall. The third and final temptation, however, receives the sort of vivid representation that was a specialty of the masque-makers. Jesus is flown "without wing / Of hippogrif" above the holy city of Jerusalem; with him, we see the towers, and "higher yet the glorious Temple . . . far off appearing like a mount / Of ala-baster." On the pinnacle, Jesus hears the words of temptation, and then come the following three lines:

> To whom thus Jesus: Also it is written,
> Tempt not the Lord thy God, he said and stood.
> But Satan smitten with amazement fell . . .
>   (4.560–62)

The one-line climax is extraordinary; it takes the astonishment that we know audiences regularly experienced at the masque transformations ("This strange spectacle gave great cause of admiration . . .")[16] and transposes it up several keys through its intense compression. Readers familiar with the biblical source material will recall that in Luke's account there is no such consequence: the next verse (4:13) reads "and when the devil had ended all the temptation, he departed from him for a season."[17] But here at once there is a dissolve to the "flowery valley" where Jesus finds a table of celestial food and drink, an image true, as those earlier ones were false. There follows a hymn, not very visual, that reaches an unexpected climax in the homely reference to the Gerasene swine. The closing four lines put events on the most modest domestic plane. There is no more mention of the throne of David. To arrive at this point in the poem with masques in mind adds remarkable depth to the reading, since the masques regularly end in a blaze of glory. How eloquent this quiet close.

This may seem no more than an amusing game, to plug the masques into the world of *Paradise Regained* and see where the poem lights up. Satan's instruments of temptation are his words and his pictures, but we note that the latter seem to define the moments

---

[16] *Coelum Britannicum*, 179.

[17] Robert P. Carroll and Stephen Prickett, eds., *The Bible: Authorized King James Version* (Oxford: Oxford Univ. Press, 1997), eBook Collection (EBSCOhost), accessed May 28, 2016, http://search.ebscohost.com/login.aspx?direct=true&scope=site&db=nlebk&db=nlabk&AN=56048. The poem may reflect some traditions of painters and sculptors here. See Roland M. Frye, *Milton's Imagery and the Visual Arts* (Princeton: PUP, 1978), chapter 4. Carey mentions also examples from Fletcher and Malory. *The Poems of John Milton*, ed. Carey and Fowler, 1164.

of greatest pressure; words do win out in the end, though, so it is tempting to equate Satan with Inigo Jones and Jesus with Ben Jonson. Although it is an entertaining thought, this is not a viable analysis, because the words that win out in the end are the words of the Hebrew scriptures. The learning of the Greeks and Romans that Jonson so revered is brutally dismissed as toys and trifles.

We may learn from the example of Jonson, however: he was working in a contentious atmosphere from early on (perhaps as early as 1612, Gordon says); moreover, he was working with a form of expression that was not classical. Everyone knows what his response was: he lectured his readers in instructive prefaces, such as the one to *Barriers at a Marriage* (1606), in which he insists on the "noble and just aduantage, that the things subiected to *understanding* haue of those which are obiected to *sense*,"[18] and in the 1616 folio, he crammed the margins with references to classical authorities. He did everything he could to evoke the kind of critical response that his contemporaries would have regarded as appropriate to the classical genres, so that the *invention* of his masques would be taken seriously and receive proper credit.

The combination of multiple discourses is something we have become used to in discussions of *Paradise Lost*, where, for instance, some passages are shown to speak of traditional patriarchy while others are shown to depict Eve as an inspiring pathfinder.[19] In his version of this exercise, Jonson brings weightier forms to bear on the slight frame of the masque; the analysis I have been proposing for *Paradise Regained* does the opposite, bringing the glamorous ephemeral appeal of color, light, and texture into a poem anchored by the forbiddingly severe worldview of Jesus. Is this too much like what Ted Turner was doing in the 1980s, when he was busy "colorizing" classic black & white movies? I hope not; in this case, I believe the colors are already there, and it is simply a matter of giving them their due. Their effect is to emphasize the attractiveness of the temptations—to us, if not to the Son of God—and, after all, for an Englishman like John Milton, looking back over the events

---

[18] *Ben Jonson*, ed. C. H. Hereford and Percy and Evelyn Simpson (Oxford: Clarendon Press, 1941), 7.209.

[19] See Joseph Wittreich, *Feminist Milton* (Ithaca, NY: Cornell Univ. Press, 1987).

of the past generation, what could better exemplify the temptation of the "kingdoms of the world" than the masques, those glittering trophies of Stuart myopia? In the heady 1640s, Milton had written "I call therefore a compleate and generous Education that which fits a man to perform justly, skilfully and magnanimously all the offices both private and publike of peace and war."[20] Satan appears to have read that passage, and to be remembering it here, in aid of what is obviously the most potent and far reaching of his three temptations. Turn stones into bread? A proposal easily resisted. Fall down and worship the Devil? Ludicrous on the face of it. But the appeal of state, of governing, of social order, the elusive notion of just and right community, of, as Satan puts it,

> Empires, and monarchs, and their radiant courts,
> Best school of best experience, quickest in sight
> In all things that to greatest actions lead.
>   (3.237–39)

—now there's real temptation.

Randolph College

---

[20] *Of Education*, Flannagan, 981.

A Protestant Pilgrim in Rome, Venice, and English Parliament: Sir John Wray

Timothy D. Crowley

S IR John Wray, second baronet of Glentworth, represented Lincolnshire in parliament once during the reign of James I and various times during that of Charles I. For his activities in the Short Parliament of 1640, we have one speech and various summaries preserved in early manuscripts.[1] His speeches from the Long Parliament of 1640–41 were printed multiple times in 1641 and show a primary concern with church reform.[2] Some of those

---

For helpful advice on drafts of this study, I thank Lara M. Crowley, Lori Anne Ferrell, Susan Green, and Donna B. Hamilton. I am also indebted to Robert C. Evans and Mary Robertson, who introduced me to Wray's *Pilgrim's Journal*; and to Reid Barbour, who introduced me to seventeenth-century English politics.

[1] See *Proceedings of the Short Parliament of 1640*, ed. Esther S. Cope and Willson H. Coates, Camden Fourth Series 19 (London: Royal Historical Society, 1977), 171, 205, 227–28, 305–6; and *The Short Parliament (1640) Diary of Sir Thomas Aston*, ed. Judith D. Maltby, Camden Fourth Series 35 (London: Royal Historical Society, 1988), 18, 19, 38, 80, 89, 95, 115, 125–26, 131. For further attention to Wray in this context, see Conrad Russell, *The Fall of the British Monarchies, 1637–1642* (Oxford: Clarendon Press, 1991), 99, 114, 118.

[2] See Sir John Wray, *Eight Occasionall Speeches, made in the House of Commons this Parliament* (London: Francis Constable, 1641); and *An Occasionall Speech made to the House of Commons this Parliament, 1641. Against Bishops. By Sir John Wray, Knight and Baronet. Being None of the 8 Speeches before Published* (London: John Nicolson, 1641). Four of these speeches were reprinted as two separate books in 1641: see Donald Wing et al.,

speeches by Wray were reprinted again decades later in context with the general proceedings.[3] On 3 May 1641, Wray characterizes himself and certain fellow parliamentarians as "holy Pilgrims." They are to be "Pilgrims" but "not Popish" he claims. They will rather be "Loyal Covenanters with God and the King"—bound, he says, "to preserve our Religion entire and pure, without the least compound of Superstition, or Idolatry."[4] Wray's characterization of himself and his parliamentary colleagues as "Covenanters" speaks to his desire for an English church more closely aligned with that of Scotland.[5] Wray's claim for the Long Parliament as a political pilgrimage, on the other hand, can be newly interpreted beyond its immediate context (analyzed at the end of this study), given the recent discovery of a travel narrative from his youth. As a young traveler, Wray had witnessed Catholic ceremonies and traditions that he considered superstitious and idolatrous. Existing biographies have not recorded precisely when and where Wray traveled; they note only that on 14 June 1604 (at 18 years of age) Wray was granted a license for three

---

Short-Title Catalogue of Books Printed in England, Scotland, Ireland, Wales, and British America, and of English Books Printed in Other Countries, 1641–1700, 2nd edition (New York: Modern Language Association of America, 1982–98), entries 3669–71A; and A. D. T. Cromartie, "The Printing of Parliamentary Speeches, November 1640–July 1642," *The Historical Journal* 33, no. 1 (1990): 23–44 (28, 30, 44).

[3] John Nalson, ed., *An Impartial Collection of the Great Affairs of State from the Beginning of the Scotch Rebellion in the Year MDCXXXIX to the Murther of King Charles I*, 2 vols. (London: Mearne et al., 1682–83), Vol. 1 (1682), 522–23, 566, 781, 786, 796–97, 809–10.

[4] Wray, *Eight Occasionall Speeches*, 12 (sig. B3*v*).

[5] This pro-Scottish bias has been recognized in biographical studies. See, James McMullen Rigg, "Wray, Sir John (1586–1655), parliamentarian," in *Dictionary of National Biography*, ed. Leslie Stephen and Sidney Lee, 21 vols. (London: Oxford Univ. Press, 1917–21; rpt. 1949–50) [*DNB*], 21:994*a*–95*a* (994*a*–*b*); David Scott, "Wray, Sir John, second baronet (bap. 1586, d. 1655), politician," in *Oxford Dictionary of National Biography*, ed. H. C. G. Matthew and Brian Harrison, 60 vols. (Oxford: Oxford Univ. Press, 2004) [*ODNB*], 60:403*b*–5*a* (404*a*–*b*). For political context, see David Stevenson, *The Scottish Revolution, 1637–1644: The Triumph of the Covenanters* (Newton Abbot: David & Charles, 1973), 214–42.

years of travel in continental Europe.[6] Recently, though, Wray's own travel account has come to light, notably titled *The Pilgrim's Journal.* By reading Wray's *Pilgrim's Journal* with an eye to his later political service, we see how his travel experience in Rome helped determine his impression of (and scorn for) all things "Popish," whereas his experience in Venice probably influenced his advocacy for tipping England's mixed government of king-in-parliament toward an increased parliamentary authority.

As a foundation for connecting Wray's Grand Tour of 1604–6 with his later parliamentary career, especially his speeches in the Long Parliament of 1640–41, this essay analyzes the rhetorical circumstances of his extant travel account from 1606, emphasizing the manner in which that manuscript text recounts his eyewitness experiences of two events in 1606: papal Easter ceremonies in Rome and the papal Interdict in Venice. Those emphases within Wray's *Pilgrim's Journal* provide an impetus for recontextualizing Wray's antagonism toward Archbishop William Laud and toward Thomas Wentworth, first Earl of Strafford. Both men were famously (or infamously) indicted for treason by the Long Parliament for their distinct exercises of power during the personal rule of Charles I, 1629–40: Laud for amplifying ecclesiastical jurisdiction to the verge of sovereignty within the English state, Strafford for his complicity in authoritarian policies and methods exercised in England and Ireland.[7] I argue that the Interdict of Venice in 1606 proved formative for Wray's perspective on English politics even before he began his political career: from the Jacobean Oath of Allegiance in 1606 to the House of Commons' Protestation and Vow and Covenant that Wray helped propose in 1641.

Wray's account of his travels between 1604 and 1606 begins with a highly self-conscious emphasis on dual motives: personal

---

[6] *Calendar of State Papers, Domestic Series, of the Reign of James I, Preserved in the State Paper Department of Her Majesty's Public Record Office,* ed. Mary Anne Everett Green, 4 vols. (London: Longman et al., 1857–59), 1:120; Charles Dalton, *History of the Wrays of Glentworth, 1523–1852,* 2 vols. (London: Chapman & Hall, 1880–81), 1:148; Rigg, "Wray," 994*a*; Scott, "Wray," 403*b*.

[7] D. Alan Orr, *Treason and the State: Law, Politics, and Ideology in the English Civil War* (Cambridge, UK: Cambridge Univ. Press, 2002), 61–140.

and political. His *Pilgrim's Journal* survives as a manuscript of
twenty small leaves, currently located in the Huntington Library.[8]
The movements it charts through France, Savoy, and Italy fit rather
closely what would become more firmly established as the typical Grand-Tour itinerary for young English gentlemen traveling
to complete their education.[9] Wray's primary visits include Paris,
Genoa, Florence, Rome, Naples (with the nearby region of Pozzuoli
and Baia), Milan, and Venice. Wray also specifies that he lived ten
months in Orleans to master French and two months in Lucca for
his Italian. The manuscript is not Wray's travel diary, nor a work
designed for a wide audience. Rather, it is a meticulously penned
account in an italic script, written shortly after his travels and presented as a gift of thanks to his father, Sir William Wray (first
baronet of Glentworth).[10] Following the dedication to his father,
Wray's text emphasizes that, in addition to acquiring languages and

---

[8] John Wray, *The Pilgrims Iournall*, Huntington Library, shelf-mark
HM60705. My citation of folio and line numbers refers to the transcription in "An Englishman on the Grand Tour, 1604–6: Sir John Wray's *Pilgrim's Journal*," ed. Timothy D. Crowley, *The Ben Jonson Journal* 9 (2002):
193–233 (197–219).

[9] For a particularly relevant survey of the context in which Wray traveled, see E. S. Bates, *Touring in 1600: A Study of the Development of Travel
as a Means of Education* (Boston: Houghton Mifflin, 1911). Modern schol-
arship associates typical Grand Tour periods with the late-seventeenth
and eighteenth centuries: see especially Christopher Hibbert, *The Grand
Tour* (New York: Putnam's Sons, 1969); Jeremy Black, *The British Abroad:
The Grand Tour in the Eighteenth Century* (New York: St. Martin's, 1992);
Edward Chaney, *The Evolution of the Grand Tour: Anglo-Italian Relations
Since the Renaissance* (Portland: Frank Cass, 1998); James Buzard, "The
Grand Tour and After (1660–1840)," in *The Cambridge Companion to
Travel Writing*, ed. Peter Hulme and Tim Youngs (Cambridge, UK: Cam-
bridge Univ. Press, 2002), 37–52; Michael G. Brennan, *English Civil War
Travellers and the Origins of the Western European Grand Tour* (London:
Hakluyt Society, 2002); Brennan, ed., *The Origins of the Grand Tour: The
Travels of Robert Montagu, Lord Mandeville, 1649–1654, William Ham-
mond, 1655–1658, Banaster Maynard, 1660–1663* (London: Hakluyt Soci-
ety, 2004); and Rosemary Sweet, *Cities and the Grand Tour: The British in
Italy, c.1690–1820* (Cambridge, UK: Cambridge Univ. Press, 2012).

[10] The dedication occurs pre-foliation: transcription in "An Englishman on the Grand Tour," ed. Crowley, 197.

witnessing the physical remains of classical antiquity, he traveled primarily to observe foreign cities' cultural, religious, and political structures—closely but cautiously. Indeed, he begins this manuscript text for his father by claiming that a "right Travailer" must carefully "garde" both "his tongue" and "his Journall": the former for the sake of self-"Preservation" and the latter for the sake of proper "observation" (fol. 1r.1–8). "Above all," Wray claims here, "let him have a care for his owne betteringe, & *his countries service*" (1r.8–9; italics added). As the eldest son of a knighted politician and wealthy landowner, young Wray anticipates regular parliamentary service like his father's, as well as the inheritance of his father's baronetcy.[11] Here in Wray's *Pilgrim's Journal*, we see a private account of his roots as a "pilgrim" for his nation's Protestant religion and parliamentary government.

Wray's preface to the *Pilgrim's Journal* conveys how his travel account is highly focused rhetorically and professionally, while also clearly a product of contemporary discourse on travel. The early modern Grand Tour entails a humanist synthesis of *gnosis* (knowledge) and *praxis* (action).[12] Perhaps Wray has consulted travel advice manuals, such as Turler's *The Traveler*.[13] Here in the early seventeenth century, Wray's venture occurs at a time of increasing interest in a "methodizing of travel."[14] In England, for instance, a manual printed in the year of Wray's return presents its commentary on aims and methods for travel in tandem with Ramist diagrams.[15] In the manuscript context of Wray's *Pilgrim's Journal*, its

---

[11] John Wray was knighted in 1612 and inherited the baronetcy of Glentworth in 1617. For a synopsis of his father's parliamentary career, see Dorothy Owen, "Wray, William (c. 1555–1617), of Glentworth, Lincs.," in *The House of Commons, 1558–1603*, ed. P. W. Hasler, 3 vols. (London: History of Parliament Trust, 1981), 3:655a–56a.

[12] Arthur F. Kinney, *Humanist Poetics: Thought, Rhetoric, and Fiction in Sixteenth-Century England* (Amherst: Univ. of Massachusetts Press, 1986), 16.

[13] Jerome Turler, *The Traveiler* (London: William How, for Abraham Veale, 1575).

[14] For this quotation and context, see Justin Stagl, *A History of Curiosity: The Theory of Travel, 1550–1800* (Chur: Harwood, 1995), 47–94.

[15] Thomas Palmer, *An essay of the meanes hovv to make our trauailes, into forraine countries, the more profitable and honourable* (London: Humphrey Lownes, for Mathew Lownes, 1606).

author's patriotic purpose proves distinct from that of printed pilgrimage accounts describing some of the same locales, such as William Lithgow's self-promotional *Painfull Peregrination* (first printed in 1614).[16] Wray chooses a travel route much more similar to that of Sir Thomas Hoby, who ventured through France and Italy in the mid-sixteenth century specifically to prepare himself for a diplomatic career and who achieved that aim with subsequent service as an English ambassador in France.[17] Wray grooms himself for parliament rather than for diplomacy, but his objectives are similar. By learning foreign languages and witnessing certain European cities' policies and customs first-hand, the young gentleman gains practical knowledge conducive to political service upon his return. Unlike the higher-profile case of Philip Sidney, both Hoby and Wray write summary narratives of their travels in France and Italy.[18]

Wray's Italian venture, like Hoby's and unlike Sidney's, takes him south into the Spanish vice-regency of Naples, where he witnesses exciting tourist curiosities and also presumably a Catholic culture more in line with Rome than with Venice. Wray goes to Spanish Naples in 1606, shortly after England's peace treaty with Spain:

---

[16] William Lithgow, *A Most Delectable, and Trve Discourse, of an Admired and Painefull Peregrination from Scotland, to the most famous Kingdomes in Europe, Asia and Affricke* (London: Nicholas Okes, for Thomas Archer, 1614). For relevant commentary on this and subsequent travel accounts by Lithgow, see Boies Penrose, *Urbane Travelers, 1591–1635* (Philadelphia: Univ. of Pennsylvania Press, 1942), 109–14, 133–35, 139–40, 155; William H. Sherman, "Stirrings and Searchings (1500–1720)," in *Cambridge Companion to Travel Writing*, ed. Hulme & Youngs, 17–36 (24, 31); Crowley, ed., "An Englishman on the Grand Tour," 228nn153–54; and Clifford Edmund Bosworth, *The Intrepid Scot: William Lithgow of Lanark's Travels in the Ottoman Lands, North Africa, and Central Europe, 1609–21* (Aldershot, UK: Ashgate, 2006), 1–36 (esp. 23–26), 130–36.

[17] See Chaney, *Evolution of the Grand Tour*, 62–63; Edgar Powell, Preface to *A Booke of the Travaile and Lief of Me Thomas Hoby*, in *The Camden Miscellany*, vol. 10, ed. Edgar Powell (London: Royal Historical Society, 1902), v–xiii; Gary M. Bell, "The Men and Their Rewards in Elizabethan Diplomatic Service, 1558–1585" (PhD thesis, UCLA, 1974), 286–90.

[18] For Sidney, see James M. Osborn, *Young Philip Sidney 1572–1577* (New Haven, CT: Yale Univ. Press, 1972); and Roger Kuin, ed. and trans., *The Correspondence of Sir Philip Sidney* (Oxford: Oxford Univ. Press, 2012).

proposed through an embassy from Spain, ratified by James I in August 1604 (two months after Wray receives his permission to travel abroad), and then finalized by Philip III of Spain in June 1605.[19] This Anglo-Spanish treaty allows a new degree of freedom for English travelers to Italy, as does the relatively open policy of Clement VIII, who is still the pope in Rome when Wray undertakes his travels.[20] Wray chooses both Spanish Milan and Spanish Naples as destinations, perhaps before leaving England or perhaps later while traveling. In 1606, he initially bypasses Rome in order to visit Naples first (fol. 6v.13–15). The city of Naples occupies less than a page of Wray's narrative, with a cursory summary of castles and council chambers plus a lively description of Neapolitan gentlemen's gallantries toward women (7r.26–27, 10–19). There is no discussion of religion here; but, as we will see below, Wray's account of Venice contrasts its tradition of religious toleration with other Italian city-states, tacitly including Naples as well as Rome. While at Naples in March 1606, Wray (like Hoby a half-century earlier) learns of famous "antiquities" and tourist "novelties" nearby in Pozzuoli and Baia, and he chooses to experience the tunnel dubbed "Virgil's tomb," the "Grotto del Can," the "Sudatoire" (a natural sauna chamber), and the "forge of Vulcan," among other attractions (7v.9–8v.15).[21] After these diversions, though, Wray rushes back from Naples to Rome for Easter Sunday (8v.16–18).

---

[19] The articles of this peace treaty were translated from Latin into English as *Articles of Peace, Entercovrse, and Commerce, Concluded in the names of the most high and mighty Kings [. . .] in a Treatie at London the 18. day of August after the Old Stile in the yeere of our Lord God 1604* (London: Robert Barker, 1605). On its negotiation from Spanish and English perspectives, see Paul C. Allen, *Philip III and the Pax Hispanica, 1598–1621* (New Haven, CT: Yale Univ. Press, 2000), 99–114; Albert J. Loomie, "Toleration and Diplomacy: The Religious Issue in Anglo-Spanish Relations, 1603–1605," *Transactions of the American Philosophical Society* 53, no. 6 (1963): 5–60; J. Duncan Mackie, "James VI and I and the Peace with Spain, 1604," *Scottish Historical Review* 23 no. 92 (1926): 241–49; and Robert W. Kenny, "Peace with Spain, 1605," *History Today* 20 (1970): 198–208.

[20] See John Walter Stoye, *English Travellers Abroad, 1604–1667: Their Influence in English Society and Politics* (London: Jonathan Cape, 1952; rpt. New York: Octagon Books, 1968), 111–12.

[21] On the *Grotta del Cane* specifically, compare Wray's *Pilgrim's Journal* (fol. 7v.17–21) with Hoby's *A Booke of the Travaile and Lief of Me*, ed.

For this Protestant pilgrim, Rome's religious pageantry is a desired spectacle, as are Rome's vestiges of classical antiquity. Perhaps to some degree, for Wray—as for other English gentlemen traveling in the late seventeenth, eighteenth, and early nineteenth centuries—personally experiencing the material remains of ancient Rome could foster distinct imperial aspirations for his own English nation.[22] Yet, if such political speculations existed in the early Jacobean period, they were far more vague and farther on the horizon than in later centuries. More immediately and cogently for this early seventeenth-century context, observing religious ceremonies could help a young Protestant English gentlemen like Wray distinguish his own Christian faith and customs of worship from those of contemporary Rome. Wray, like Hoby before him, provides wry criticism of papal authority and Catholic custom.[23] Wray's account of Rome is more lively and sarcastic in tone, probably due to its rhetorical context. In writing the *Pilgrim's Journal* for his father after his travels, Wray's tone bespeaks his identity. This portion on Rome provides a detailed description of those foreign religious observances

---

Powell, 31; and see Antoni Maczak, *Travel in Early Modern Europe*, trans. Ursula Phillips (Oxford: Blackwell/Polity Press, 1995), 193–95, 273–75. On legends attached to the *Grotta* dubbed *Virgiliana*, see J. B. Trapp, "The Grave of Vergil," *Journal of the Warburg and Courtauld Institutes* 47 (1984): 1–31.

[22] On those later contexts in this regard, see Buzard, "The Grand Tour and After," 40; and Sweet, *Cities and the Grand Tour*, 99, 126–27, 129 (cf. 129–31, 160–63). For a similar perspective voiced by an English ambassador to Venice upon visiting Rome in the early seventeenth century, see Stoye, *English Travellers Abroad*, 122.

[23] For Hoby's perspective, see especially his commentary on papal indulgences granted for the Jubilee year of 1550 (*Travaile and Lief*, ed. Powell, 60–61). On Hoby's account of Rome and circumstances in Italy, analyzed in tandem with those of his fellow English traveler William Thomas, see Brett Foster, "The Metropolis of Popery: Writing of Rome in the English Renaissance" (PhD thesis, Yale University, 2005), 14–91; and Jonathan Woolfson, "Thomas Hoby, William Thomas, and Mid-Tudor Travel to Italy," in *The Oxford Handbook of Tudor Literature*, ed. Mike Pincombe and Cathy Shrank (Oxford: Oxford Univ. Press, 2009), 404–17 (410–13; cf. 415 on the composition of Hoby's extant manuscript account). For further context, see Brennan, ed., *Origins of the Grand Tour*, 9–13.

that repel him. For Wray, the idea of the Grand Tour, like that of traditional religious pilgrimage, involves primarily a reinforcement of preexisting knowledge and beliefs through travel experience.

Wray's eyewitness account of Rome at Easter in 1606 deploys a variety of tones to criticize the Catholic rites that he deems superstitious and idolatrous. Sometimes he critiques with ironic hyperbole, as in his attention to the matter of religious indulgences associated with pious devotion at the *Scala Sancta* (fol. 10*v*.18–11*r*.1). On those thirty steps associated with Christ's Passion, Wray claims snidely that, for a Catholic devotee, merely climbing them to gain the indulgences

> is not sufficient penⁿance, for he must say vpon every steppe a Pater noster & Ave Maria, for wᶜʰ oraisons he obtaines soe many 20 yeares pardon for all the sinⁿes venall or mortall, he shall comⁿitt in 3 hundreth yeares after. (10*v*.24–11*r*.1)

Other times he attacks Roman Catholics more bluntly, capping his short description of St. Peter's Basilica, for instance, with the synopsis that it contained "an infinitye of other relickes after whⁱch I made no inquiry supposing these are sufficient to testifye their blinde & willfull ignorance" (11*r*.4–5). Wray uses a similar tone in scoffing at certain actions by Pope Paul V, who had been elected recently (16 May 1605) during Wray's travels in France. For example, he refers to the indulgences distributed by this pope on each Sunday of Lent as "recul'de Papisticall maledictions" (11*v*.6): that is, papal curses eagerly collected by the Roman populace as if they were blessings.[24] While defining that papal custom as a "very solemne Antichristiall procession" (11*r*.22), Wray's *Pilgrim's Journal* describes the spectacle in great detail (11*r*.20–11*v*.6). Even more detail pervades the ensuing account of Pope Paul V's distinct procession to St. Peter's Basilica for the Easter Sunday Mass, including precise vocabulary for ecclesiastical vestments (11*v*.6–13). Wray describes the pope's consecration of the Eucharist with equal precision:

> washinge his hands, he receives of one of the Cardinalls his Host, whⁱch devoutly consecratinge he elevates in like manⁿer the

---

[24] Cf. *Oxford English Dictionary*, "recueil, *v.*": 1. *trans.* "to gather together, collect."

> Callice [chalice] of which he drincketh thrise, then rincinge the
> cup with a litle water, he powres it vpon his naile, which he suckes
> as loth to leave a dropp of soe pretious a liquor. (11v.14–18)

Here Wray critiques the Catholic doctrine of transubstantiation
with an irony much more subtle than that of his hyperbole regarding indulgences.

Wray infuses his account of Rome with a more sarcastic irony
in shifting focus from the religious ceremonies to civic policies and
Roman *mores* more generally. As "a good testimony of the libertye
of their religion," he critiques the behavior of the Vatican's Cardinals amid their procession each Sunday, wherein, Wray claims,
these church leaders "salute every Curtizan [courtesan] that looks
out at her windowe, & sometime not ashamed to goe publickly
into their Burdellos" (fol. 12r.6–10). According to Wray's account,
the "liberty" of Roman culture, which he associates directly with
Catholicism in general, consists not only of loose morals but also
of greed. In conceding, for example, that "they say the Pope hath
tried all meanes to punish those ordinary Putani [whores]," Wray
emphasizes that prostitution remains "profitable" to the papacy
through taxation:

> In Rome there are about some tenne thousand weomen of
> y^t stuffe, vnto whom the Pope (in a good thrifty & no lesse
> catholicke consideration) hath given free liberty to vse their trade;
> Alwaies provided they pay yearely a certain trifle for renuinge of
> their freedome. (12r.10–16).

The satirical edge of Wray's narrative touches upon politics
when he describes the rites of humility and "thanksgivinge to *Saint*
Peter" displayed by Pope Paul V in receiving the papal tiara as a
"Crowne" of office (fol. 11v.18–23). Wray concludes this section
with obvious sarcasm regarding a customary conclave of Cardinals
held on Easter Monday, wherein the pope

> treates of all Ecclesiasticall Negotiations, as well forreine as
> domesticke, He sits then in *Saint* Peters chaire where they holde
> he canot erre, there he makes Bulles, gives indulgences, excommunicates Princes, And disposeth of the severall rooms of Paradice, & Purgatorie at his pleasure, Blame him not for he keeps y^e
> keyes of both places. (11v.24–12r.2)

Within the context of Wray's *Pilgrim's Journal,* this passage resonates quite obviously with the sarcasm he voices elsewhere regarding Roman Catholic faith. Yet its reference to "excommunicat[ing] Princes" also addresses a topical event related later in Wray's text: a political and religious conflict between Rome and Venice the following month of this same year, while Wray was in Venice. We must remember that Wray composed these accounts of Rome and Venice together after his travels.

For readers of *The Pilgrim's Journal,* Wray's sarcasm here regarding papal claims of authority serves as an implicit foundation for his later commendation of Leonardo Donato (Donà), the current Doge of Venice. After Wray outlines in detail the structure of the Venetian republic, he notes that Donato had been elected only very recently (fol. 15*v*.4–16*r*.11).[25] Already, an ongoing Venetian conflict with Rome had reached its apex. While Wray was there in April 1606, news came from Rome that Pope Paul V excommunicated the entire Venetian senate and declared the city to be under interdict: that is, forbidding the seven sacraments to be administered. These papal actions responded to the Venetian senate's insistence on balancing ecclesiastical and secular rights in the acquisition, taxation, and sale of land and property, as well as in legal procedure with allegations against certain clergymen.[26] Wray's *Pilgrim's Journal* evaluates the new Doge of Venice's reaction to the news as heroic:

> at y^t time when we were in Venice vpon the first report of ye Popes Breve [i.e., papal edict], & their [i.e., the Venetian senate's] excom*m*unication, this Prince tooke it in such scorne, as even then he gave publicke testimonye, y^t he neither feared his maledictions, nor valued his Benedictions. (16*r*.13–16)

---

[25] Wray claims March 1606 (fol. 16*r*.10), but the election had occurred earlier in January 1606.

[26] See William J. Bouwsma, *Venice and the Defense of Republican Liberty: Renaissance Values in the Age of the Counter Reformation* (Berkeley: Univ. of California Press, 1968), 339–482 (esp. 339–40, 347–49, 355–56, 363–64, 372–73, 382, 387, 417–20, 481–82). A concise recent synopsis of these causes appears in Filippo de Vivo, *Information and Communication in Venice: Rethinking Early Modern Politics* (Oxford: Oxford Univ. Press, 2007), 157–59 (see 157–99, 244–51, on this Interdict of 1606–7).

In Wray's view, Donato's opposition to papal bombast entails "pro-founde iudgement of an acute apprehension, & of a stoute resolution" (16r.11–12).[27]

Such strong leadership provokes one of Wray's many praises for the Venetian republic. With approbation, for instance, he defines Venice's *Gran Collegia* of elected representatives as "ye bodye of the Signorie, who *iointly together with their Prince* [i.e., the Doge] have absolute power to dispose & governe the frame of their Commonwealth" (fol. 16r.8–9; italics added). Wray commends this particular Venetian regime for a perceived policy of moderation in meting out death sentences: "the Signorie will hardly or rarely condemne a man to death vnlesse it be for some offe[n]ce or iniurie offered to the State" (16v.27–17r.1). This emphasis on secular justice serves as a springboard for his primary admiration of the Venetian commonwealth: its religious toleration. As Wray puts it, pithily, "there is no inquisition for matter of conscience" (17r.3). He makes sure to highlight this degree of toleration as unique among Italian city states (16v.25–27). Here we should bear in mind the inquisitional institutions of Rome and of Spanish Milan and Spanish Naples, where Wray also traveled. Within Venice and its territories, on the other hand, Wray claims that as a traveler you may "doe what you will[;] soe you touch not the state no man will trouble you" (17r.4–5). Wray buys into Venice's almost mythical status as a commonwealth, claiming that the Venetian republic has outlasted the ancient Roman Empire due to the stability of its civic policies:

> this renowned Republicke or Commonwealth of Venice hath by it[s] wisedome & civill policy vphelde it selfe now 12 hundreth years, beionde the Period of the Romaine Monarchy, which testifies their invincible vnion & their inviolable observation of lawes, which provided they be diligently executed are ye only meanes

---

[27] Donato served as the celebrant for Catholic masses and even ordained new priests during this liminal period of the interdict, May 1606–April 1607 (Bouwsma, *Venice*, 387; cf. 255, 433). On the Venetian government's policy of emphasizing ritual amid the sacramental restriction, see Vivo, *Information and Communication*, 170–76 (cf. 244).

to keepe each member in order & conserve the tranquility of the whole bodye. (17r.23–17v.2)[28]

To support this observation, in proper humanist fashion, Wray concludes this commentary with a quotation from classical Rome: "as well saith Sallust: Concordia Parvae res crescent, Discordia vero maxima dilabuntur" (17v.9–11).[29]

At this point in the *Pilgrim's Journal*, between these summary comments on Venice and the quotation from Sallust, Wray provides a brief digression wherein we see the seeds of his later political activity. "[I]n diverse other Monarchies," Wray claims,

> soe soone as some *vnruly heifers puft vp with ambitions crust*, woulde overwhelme obedience[,] the wheele of lawes, from thence have sprunge the cruell furies of civill dissentions vsurpinge the place of vnion & concorde y^t before gave them lustre. (fol. 17v.5–9; emphasis added)

Here, immediately before the quotation from Sallust, Wray's impassioned diction suggests that this comment may be more than just a product of his classical learning. Wray's prefatory letter to his father and his use of phrases such as "my late pilgrimadge" (4r.9) indicate that he wrote his *Pilgrim's Journal* shortly after his return to England in May 1606. He most likely composed the text and delivered it to his father in the summer of 1606. In that context, amid Wray's comments on "the observation of lawes," his reference to

---

[28] For similar praise of Venice, see the English ambassador Henry Wotton's speech of 16 January 1606 on the occasion of Donato's election as Doge six days earlier (Logan Pearsall Smith, *The Life and Letters of Sir Henry Wotton*, 2 vols. [Oxford: Clarendon Press, 1907], 1:54; cf. Bouwsma, *Venice*, 355–56). While in Venice, Wray almost certainly would have met Wotton, who probably served as Wray's tour guide and, given Wray's social position, might have hosted the young traveler at his home (cf. Smith, *Life and Letters*, 1:60). On Wotton and the interdict of 1606, see Smith, *Life and Letters*, 1:78–86; Bouwsma, *Venice*, 392–93; and Stoye, *English Travellers Abroad*, 148–49.

[29] See Sallust, *Bellum Iugurthinum* 10.6, which R. C. Rolfe translates, "for harmony makes small states great, while discord undermines the mightiest empires" (*Sallust*, Loeb Classical Library [Cambridge, MA: Harvard Univ. Press, 1931]).

"vnruly heifers puft vp with ambitions crust" would have evoked the foiled Gunpowder Plot that occurred while Wray traveled, in relation to James I's controversial insistence thereafter on the Oath of Allegiance, implemented as law in June 1606. When Wray penned the emphasis on "obedience" as essential for "vnion & concorde" in relation to "civil dissentions," it seems likely that he bore in mind his English king's Oath of Allegiance: perhaps interpreting it as an early effort to preempt future attempts at civil insurrection with a new gesture toward religious toleration.[30]

Wray's travel experience in Italy allowed him to witness in Venice's republic a balance between religious toleration and a strong sovereign figurehead. In his view, at least as of 1606, both were conducive to civil obedience, and both were essential to counteract corrupt ecclesiastical authority like that of Rome. Such an awareness of Venetian liberty and stability probably influenced his and many other English parliamentarians' emphasis on religious toleration as a crucial political issue in the early seventeenth century.[31] Decades later in the Long Parliament, amid Wray's speeches on religious reform and the English monarchy, we hear a more clearly articulated ideological consciousness that resonates intriguingly with that voiced within his *Pilgrim's Journal* on the contrast between Venetian and Roman government.

---

[30] For interpretive debate in modern historiography, see Michael C. Questier, "Loyalty, Religion, and State Power in Early Modern England: English Romanism and the Jacobean Oath of Allegiance," *The Historical Journal* 40 (1997): 311–29; Johann P. Sommerville, "Papalist Political Thought and the Controversy Over the Jacobean Oath of Allegiance," in *Catholics and the "Protestant Nation": Religion, Politics, and Identity in Early Modern England,* ed. Ethan Shagan (Manchester, UK: Manchester Univ. Press, 2005), 162–84; Questier, "Catholic Loyalism in Early Stuart England," *English Historical Review* 123, no. 504 (2008): 1132–65. On European contexts, see Charles H. McIlwain, ed., *Political Works of James I* (Cambridge, MA: Harvard Univ. Press, 1918), xlix–lxxx; and W. B. Patterson, *King James VI and I and the Reunion of Christendom* (Cambridge, MA: Cambridge Univ. Press, 1997), 75–123.

[31] Conrad Russell makes a more general claim about travel experience and English parliamentarians' concern for religious toleration, tied to France and the Low Countries rather than to Venice (*Unrevolutionary England, 1603–1642* [London: Hambledon, 1990], 199).

As a bridge between these different contexts of 1606 and 1641, it proves useful to contrast Wray's experiences as a traveler and a politician with those of the English peer whose execution for treason Wray promoted assiduously in the Long Parliament: Sir Thomas Wentworth, first Earl of Strafford. Wentworth's account of his activities and of the books he acquired in France as a young man suggests that even in 1611–12 he was attentive to foreign justifications of absolute monarchy.[32] This aspect of Wentworth's political thought helped to inform his later political actions. It is worthwhile to note that Wray represented Grimsby in the Addled Parliament of 1614, wherein he would have known about Wentworth, already then a bold and controversial figure.[33] In the Parliament of 1628, as a precursor to Wray's future opposition of Wentworth, Wray spoke against the Duke of Buckingham as an example of the nationally corrupting influence of royal favoritism.[34] When Wentworth served as Lord Deputy of Ireland in the 1630s, he supported the authoritarian religious and political agendas of Archbishop Laud and of King Charles I. By 1640, when Wentworth was elevated to the earldom of Strafford and to the position of Lord Lieutenant in Ireland, he, like Laud, had become an incendiary public figure. Amid the Long Parliament's debates about religious reform, royal privileges, and royal counsel in 1640–41, the controversy surrounding Strafford was amplified, both within Parliament and within the public sphere at large. He was impeached by a motion from the House

---

[32] Stoye, *English Travellers Abroad*, 64–66.

[33] For Wray, see Mary Frear Keeler, *The Long Parliament, 1640–1641: A Biographical Study of Its Members* (Philadelphia: American Philosophical Society, 1954), 400*b*–401*a* (401*a*, at note 574). For Wentworth, see David Colclough, "'Better Becoming a Senate of Venice'?: The 'Addled Parliament' and Jacobean Debates on Freedom of Speech," in *The Crisis of 1614 and The Addled Parliament: Literary and Historical Perspectives*, ed. Stephen Clucas and Rosalind Davies (Aldershot, UK: Ashgate, 2002), 51–61 (52–55).

[34] For the relevant quotation with a citation of the manuscript witness, see Clive Holmes, *Seventeenth-Century Lincolnshire* (Lincoln: Society for Lincolnshire History & Archaeology, 1980), 104. For a general perspective on Wray in this context with regard to Wentworth, see Conrad Russell, *Parliaments and English Politics, 1621–1629* (Oxford: Clarendon Press, 1979), 17, 376.

of Commons, investigated in the House of Lords on complex and inconclusive allegations of treason, indicted by the House of Commons with a Bill of Attainder, and then executed as a scapegoat with the reluctant consent of Charles I.[35] In this heated parliamentary context, Wray's speeches argue for radical church reform that would protect England from the authoritarian policies of Strafford and Laud, ultimately promoting a revised model of king-in-parliament.

Wray supported the indictments of Strafford and of Laud primarily for religious reasons. His speeches convey an interest in closer religious ties between England and Scotland, with a target focus (as a recent biographer puts it) "somewhere between a 'primitive' [English] episcopacy and [a] Scottish-style presbyterianism."[36] His arguments highlight an ancient liberty of the English people tied to the Magna Carta, together with the uniquely English sixteenth-century innovation of a Protestant church led politically and

---

[35] Bibliography on Strafford and these contexts is extensive. See, for instance, Orr, *Treason and the State*, 61–100; Ronald G. Asch, "Wentworth, Thomas, first earl of Strafford (1593–1641), lord lieutenant of Ireland," in *ODNB*, 58:142–57; David Stevenson, *Scottish Covenanters and Irish Confederates: Scottish-Irish Relations in the Mid-Seventeenth Century* (Belfast: Ulster Historical Foundation, 1981), 1–41; Robert Wilcher, *The Writing of Royalism, 1628–1660* (Cambridge, UK: Cambridge Univ. Press, 2001), 3–4, 21–89; Russell, *Unrevolutionary England*, 89–109, 179–204 (esp. 199); Russell, *Fall of the British Monarchies*, 274–302; Terence Kilburn and Anthony Milton, "The Public Context of the Trial and Execution of Strafford," in *The Political World of Thomas Wentworth, Earl of Strafford, 1621–1641*, ed. J. F. Merritt (Cambridge, UK: Cambridge Univ. Press, 1996), 230–51; and Elizabeth Sauer, *"Paper-Contestations" and Textual Communities in England, 1640–1675* (Toronto: University of Toronto Press, 2005), 35–56.

[36] Scott, "Wray," 404a. Here this *ODNB* entry revises the *DNB* entry, which characterizes Wray as a "zealous presbyterian" (Rigg, "Wray," 994a). Drawing upon a different source base (private commentary on religious patronage), J. T. Cliffe claims that Wray "is said to have viewed with equal repugnance both prelacy and Presbyterianism" (*The Puritan Gentry: The Great Puritan Families of Early Stuart England* [London: Routledge & Kegan Paul, 1984], 184). This characterization fits Scott's emphasis that Wray's primary aversion was to prelacy.

spiritually by the monarch.[37] Herein lies the basis for Wray's claims against both Strafford and Laud as corrupting influences on religious policy under Charles I. In November 1640, for instance, Wray called for "a thorough Reformation" that would "lay the Axe to the root, to unloose the long and deep Fangs of Superstition and Popery" in England.[38] Less than a month later, Wray specified that he means not necessarily to abolish all episcopal offices but rather to expel dangerously "proud" bishops in the tradition of Beckett and Wolsey, who tyrannously command "their tottering Hierarchy . . . built with untempered morter."[39] Metaphorically, Wray deploys the word "mortar" here both as building material and as artillery, the military innuendo relevant to this speech's focus on contesting Archbishop Laud's controversial ecclesiastical canons issued in May of that year. Wray concludes the speech with more overt wordplay to that effect. Religious unity, he claims, "will never bee safe, nor well at quiet, untill these heavie drossy Cannons with all their base mettle, be melted, and desolved: let us then dismount them, and destroy them, which is my humble motion."[40] By disabling the archbishop's canons, Wray and his compatriots could assault the crumbling walls of his ecclesiastical sovereignty within England. In January 1641, Wray voiced his Anglo-Scottish sympathies more overtly in arguing

---

[37] These premises appear most clearly in Wray, *An Occasionall Speech . . . Against Bishops*. On rhetorical context for Wray's premises about bishops and Magna Carta, see Russell, *Fall of the British Monarchies*, 194.

[38] Wray, *Eight Occasionall Speeches*, 4 (sig. A3*v*); see pp. 1–5. On Wray within the rhetorical context of root-and-branch debate for religious reform, see George Yule, *Puritans in Politics: The Religious Legislation of the Long Parliament, 1640–1647* ([Abingdon, UK]: Sutton Courtenay Press, 1981), 106–25 (114); Cliffe, *Puritan Gentry*, 220–23, 230; Scott, "Wray," 404*a*. On Wray and the House of Commons' Root and Branch Bill of 1641, see Russell, *Fall of the British Monarchies*, 344–45. On this context, also see Julie Fann, "Presbyterian Church and State Before *The Solemn League and Covenant*," *Renaissance Papers 2007* (2008): 33–54 (50–53).

[39] Wray, *Eight Occasionall Speeches*, pp. 6, 5 (sig. A4*r–v*).

[40] Wray, *Eight Occasionall Speeches*, p. 7 (sig. B1*r*). Helen Pierce has noted Wray's wordplay with cannons/canons ("Anti-Episcopacy and Graphic Satire in England, 1640–1645," *The Historical Journal* 47, no. 4 [2004]: 809–48 [821]). On Wray in this political context, see Russell, *Fall of the British Monarchies*, 233–34.

for an English concession to end the second Bishops' War.[41] Then, as the Long Parliament continued, Wray targeted several speeches at the Earl of Strafford as an obstacle to any such resolution of armed conflict.[42]

In the case of King Charles I, Wray argued for revising England's government of church and state, toward a new covenant between king and parliament. Here we return to Wray's speech from 3 May 1641, wherein he defines himself and his fellow parliamentarians in the House of Commons as "holy Pilgrims" in the following manner:

> If ever wee intend to perfect and finish the great works we have begun, and come to our journey's end, let us take and follow the right way, which is *Via tuta*; and that is in a word to become holy Pilgrims, not Popish, and to endeavour to be loyall Covenanters with God and the King; first binding our selves by a Parliamentary and Nationall Oath, (not a Straffordian, nor a Prelaticall one) to preserve our Religion entire and pure, without the least compound of Superstition, or Idolatry: next, to defend the Defender of the Faith, his Royall person, Crowne, and dignity, and maintaine our Soveraigne in his glory and splendor, which can never be eclipsed, if the ballance of justice goe right, and his lawes be duly executed.
>
> Thus doing, Mr. *Speaker*, and making Jerusalem our chiefest joy, we shall be a blessed Nation, and a happy People. But if we shall let goe our Christian hold, and loose our Parliament proofe, and old English well-tempered mettle; let us take heed that our Buckler break not, our Parliaments melt not, and our golden Candlestick be not removed; which let me never live to see, nor *England* to feele the want of: that is my prayer to conclude my former motion.[43]

---

[41] Wray, *Eight Occasionall Speeches*, 7–8 (sig. B1*r–v*); Russell, *Fall of the British Monarchies*, 187. On Wray's complementary perspective in November 1640, see John Morrill, "The Religious Context of the English Civil War," *Transactions of the Royal Historical Society* [5th Series] 34 (1984): 155–78 (155–56); and Russell, *Fall of the British Monarchies*, 174n94 (cf. 166).

[42] Wray, *Eight Occasionall Speeches*, 8–12 (sig. B1*v*–B3*v*).

[43] Wray, *Eight Occasionall Speeches*, 12–13 (sig. B3*v*–B4*r*).

When Wray characterizes himself and his fellow parliamentarians not only as "holy Pilgrims" but also as "loyal Covenanters with God and the King," he applies the metaphor of pilgrimage to the new political and religious oaths known as the Protestation and Vow and Covenant, first proposed this same day (3 May 1641). Wray and other parliamentarians with Scottish sympathies designed this Protestation and introduced it by means of a comparison to the parliamentary Bond of Association in 1584, which established an oath of loyalty to Elizabeth I against potential Catholic conspiracies.[44]

Wray builds upon his earlier speeches against Strafford and Laud by emphasizing that this Protestation would constitute "a Parliamentary and National oath (not a Straffordian, nor a Prelatical one) to preserve our Religion entire and pure, without the least compound of Superstition, or Idolatry." This speech gives new context to the "golden Candlestick" reference that Wray had deployed the previous December in his speech against Laud, associating the Long Parliament's new trajectory for the Church of England with one of the seven candlesticks featured in the Book of Revelation. Wray probably drew this apocalyptic imagery from the work of

---

[44] Edward Vallance, "'An Holy and Sacramentall Paction': Federal Theology and the Solemn League and Covenant in England," *English Historical Review* 116, no. 465 (2001): 50–75 (52, 60–61). On Wray in this context, also see Holmes, *Seventeenth-Century Lincolnshire*, 143–44 (cf. 139–40); Morrill, "Religious Context," 170–73; Russell, *Fall of the British Monarchies*, 294–95; and Scott, "Wray," 404*b*. Nalson provides the Protestation's text and a list of those in the House of Commons who signed it: Nalson, ed., *An Impartial Collection of the Great Affairs of State*, 810–13. On the parliamentary transactions of this day (3 May 1641), also see *Proceedings in the Open Session of the Long Parliament: House of Commons, Volume 4: 19 April–5 June 1641*, ed. Maija Jansson [with Alisa Plant] (Rochester: Univ. of Rochester Press, 2003), 169–83. On the 1584 legislation mentioned by Vallance, see David Dean, *Law-Making and Society in Late Elizabethan England: The Parliament of England, 1584–1601* (Cambridge, UK: Cambridge Univ. Press, 1996), 63–65; David Cressy, "Binding the Nation: The Bonds of Association, 1584 and 1696," in *Tudor Rule and Revolution*, eds. Delloyd J. Guth and John W. McKenna (Cambridge, UK: Cambridge Univ. Press, 1982), 217–34 (217–26, 233–34); Jonathan M. Gray, "So Help Me God: Oaths and the English Reformation" (PhD thesis, Stanford University, 2008), 446–56.

Robert Parker, who already had published *The Seaven Golden Candlesticks* in 1621 and then gave a manuscript of his *The Ready Way to
Good Works* to Sir John Wray as its dedicatee.[45] In this new context
of 3 May 1641, Wray adds that the Long Parliament's root-and-
branch reform must also "defend the Defender of the Faith" in a
manner that does "justice" to England's long tradition of "balance"
between monarchs, lords, and parliament. Wray's reference to "our
journey's end" as *"Via tuta"* quotes directly from his speech against
Strafford a month earlier, wherein he emphasizes that from this historical moment Strafford's execution must ensue: they have the wolf
by the ears, and this is the only way to rid the country of its danger.[46] Wray had deployed this same rhetoric of urgency about "the
way of truth: *Via tuta*" in his speech against Laud on 15 December
1640, just three days before the archbishop's imprisonment.[47] He
does so again on 3 May 1641 to support the Protestation levied that
day as part of an agenda to expedite the Bill of Attainder against
Strafford, who is already in prison.

By reconstructing Wray's place within this political moment, we
find further justification for my speculation above that Wray alludes
indirectly to the Gunpowder Plot when writing his 1606 account of
Venice in contrast with Rome. A detailed contemporary account of
Strafford's final days claims that Wray had in mind the Gunpowder
Plot there, too, thirty-five years later. On the morning of 3 May
1641, the House Speaker John Pym announced his knowledge of
the Army Plot, involving a military invasion of the Tower designed
to free Strafford and possibly also to terminate the Long Parliament.
This announcement may mark an important transition in policy for
Pym, who, up to this point, had coordinated negotiations among
the king, the Scots, and the English Parliament. Pym and Wray
shared similar perspectives on religious reform in England and on
Anglo-Scottish alliance; but, unlike Wray, Pym had unsuccessfully
opposed the House of Commons' transition from impeachment of

---

[45] See Cliffe, *Puritan Gentry*, 221, 274n23 (cf. 206–7).

[46] These portions of both speeches appear in Wray, *Eight Occasionall
Speeches*, 12 (sig. B3*v*).

[47] Wray, *Eight Occasionall Speeches*, 6 (sig. A4*r*).

Strafford to attainder.[48] As a prosecutor, Pym sought to cultivate common interest between Charles I and Parliament. In mid-April, for instance, he argued that Strafford's authoritarian exercises of power had constituted treason in subverting English law's protection of the monarch and the state.[49] Yet, here in early May, when Pym perceived Charles I's complicity in the Army Plot, his efforts at conciliation ended: from this point we suddenly find (as Conrad Russell puts it) "no evidence of serious negotiation between Pym and the king."[50] Parliament acted to prevent its own dissolution were the king to order it. Wray and his associates introduced the oath of Protestation, both rhetorically as a new religious Covenant between the king and his people, and politically as a means to protect the state against Catholic invasion.[51] This day and the next, rumor and hysteria about the Army Plot spread throughout London, including protests by prominent citizens outside the House of Lords, pressuring them to advance the Bill of Attainder against Strafford. During these two days, a shift in political power occurred, whereby Parliament usurped the king's authority by levying military forces. Already by May 4, Strafford had written his famous letter releasing Charles I from an earlier royal pledge of loyalty, thereby setting himself up for his own execution as a scapegoat. According to an eyewitness account by a parliamentary clerk, here on May 5, at the height of these crisis circumstances, while Pym communicated the full extent of what he knew about supposed Catholic invasion plots, a floorboard in the House of Commons' gallery cracked as MPs stood up, and Sir John Wray claimed that he smelled gunpowder. The Commons fled outdoors, and this incident caused the temporary muster of one military band that day.[52] Such was the Gunpowder Plot's cultural currency decades after the event.

---

[48] Conrad Russell, "Pym, John (1584–1643), politician," in *ODNB*, 45:624*b*–40*a* (637*a–b*); Scott, "Wray," 404*a–b*.

[49] Orr, *Treason and the State*, 96–97.

[50] Russell, "Pym," 637*b*.

[51] Conrad Russell, "The First Army Plot of 1641," *Transactions of the Royal Historical Society* 38 (1988): 85–106 (104–5); cf. Russell, *Fall of the British Monarchies*, 294–96.

[52] John Rushworth, *The Tryal of Thomas, Earl of Strafford* (London: for John Wright and Richard Chiswell, 1680), 744–45; John H. Timmis, III,

The eyewitness account of Wray's action on 5 May 1641 imbues it with agency in contributing to the day's political panic. John Rushworth's *The Trial of Thomas, Earl of Strafford*, published in 1680 but rooted in Rushworth's clerical notes from the Long Parliament, claims,

> Sir *Walter Earl* was making a Report to the House of some Plot and Design to blow up the House of Commons; Whereupon, some Members in the Gallery stood up, the better to hear the Report, and Mr. *Moyle* of *Cornwal*, and Mr. *Middleton* of *Sussex*, two persons of good bigness, weighed down a board in the Gallery, which gave so great a crack, that some Members thought it was a Plot indeed; and Sir *John Wray* speaking out, he smelt Gunpowder, hastening back out of the Gallery; some Members and others in fear, running out of the House, frighted people in the *Lobby*, who ran into the Hall, crying out, *The Parliament House was falling, and the Members were slain.*[53]

Rushworth's historiography on Strafford's trial, claiming on its title page to be "impartial," complements his ongoing Historical Collections (1659–1700), a multi-volume documentary history of the English civil war beginning (controversially for royalists) in 1618. As a royalist response to early volumes of Rushworth's documentary historiography, John Nalson's Impartial Collection of the Great Affairs of State appeared in 1682–83. Faithfully reprinting Wray's speeches from the Long Parliament, Nalson's edition claims that as early as 26 February 1641 Wray and other prosecutors felt "insecure of their own lives" due to "fear of [Strafford's] innocence, and the necessity of making him appear Criminal."[54] Nalson frames Wray's speech on 3 May 1641 with an emphasis that at this point Wray and his associates aimed "to Establish themselves in a Sovereign and boundless Authority of sitting so long as they pleased themselves . . . without the Consent of the King and Lords, or so much as their Privity, and a kind of Combination or Covenant to discriminate

---

Thine Is the Kingdome: The Trial for Treason of Thomas Wentworth, Earl of Strafford (Tuscaloosa: University of Alabama Press, 1974), 160–65 (163); cf. Russell, *Fall of the British Monarchies*, 293–300.

[53] Rushworth, *Tryal*, 744.

[54] Nalson, ed., *An Impartial Collection of the Great Affairs of State*, 781.

their Party and try their Strength."[55] This accusation clearly constitutes Tory polemic. Rushworth's own position is more difficult to determine. From extant witnesses to his methodology, including copious shorthand notes in volumes from his library of sources from the 1630s and 1640s, we can infer that, generally speaking, Rushworth compared and assessed diverse sources rather than relying on his own notes and memory alone.[56] The precise details of cracking floorboards and Wray crying wolf seem idiosyncratic. Perhaps Rushworth invented them as dramatic embellishments. Perhaps not. Wray's persistent antagonism of Strafford would put him in a vulnerable position, as Nalson claims, were Strafford to be freed from the Tower and Parliament dissolved. Regarding Wray's agency and motives in early May of 1641, both Rushworth's and Nalson's accounts seem plausible.

Here in May 1641, perhaps Wray capitalized strategically upon a similar degree of paranoia that he probably witnessed both at home and abroad in 1606. For instance, in the immediate wake of Pope Paul V's actions against Venice, England's resident ambassador Sir Henry Wotton (who, as mentioned above, probably hosted young Wray in Venice) claimed that an international Jesuit conspiracy motivated both the Interdict of Venice and the previous year's Gunpowder Plot in England.[57] With the Protestation of 1641, Wray might have remembered the Venetian *Protesto* of 6 May 1606, authored by Paolo Sarpi and widely publicized as a preemptive strike against the papal interdict less than a week before it was to take effect. Issued in the name of Doge Donato, this *Protesto* had claimed for him and the republic a divine right in governance for the public good.[58] In that earlier context, James I of England had supported Venetian sovereignty over papal intrusion, and he emphasized the matter of sovereign authority as crucial for

---

[55] Nalson, ed., *An Impartial Collection of the Great Affairs of State*, 809, 810.

[56] Frances Henderson, "'Posterity to Judge': John Rushworth and His *Historical Collections*," *Bodleian Library Record* 15 (1996): 247–59 (254–56).

[57] See Smith, *Life and Letters*, 80 (cf. 81 on James I); and note 28 above.

[58] See Vivo, *Information and Communication*, 166–67.

political stability across Europe and at home in Britain.[59] Based on Wray's rhetoric in 1641 about the English tradition of a king-in-parliament, modern biography may be right in characterizing him as both "more of a religious enthusiast than an enemy to the King" and "more of a religious enthusiast than a republican."[60] Yet, neither of the kings he served upon his return to England evoked from him any such praise as that which he afforded the Doge of Venice in 1606. Under Charles I, Wray's parliamentary speeches consistently attacked royal favoritism as dangerous to the nation's laws and religion: first with Buckingham in 1628, then with Strafford in 1641. When Wray proposes a new Covenant between "God and the king" on 3 May 1641, with the "king" portion perhaps he was hedging his bets as an adamant supporter of Strafford's imminent execution. If he did indeed claim to smell gunpowder in the House of Commons on 5 May 1641, it was with a dramatic intent to fan the flames of a current political crisis.

However we interpret Wray in relation to Charles I at this historical moment, it seems clear that Parliament, and the House of Commons in particular, was Wray's political priority. As in the *Pilgrim's Journal* of 1606, here in May 1641 Wray condoned a singular political figurehead as the leader of a collective governing body that protects the public's religious liberty from authoritarian ecclesiastical power. Although this Protestant reformer wrote his *Pilgrim's Journal* only shortly after his return to England, its account of Venice suggests that Wray's travels already had provoked a critical contemplation of his own nation's laws in 1606. In his commentary there on "obedience" as "the wheele of lawes" (fol. 17*v*.7), Wray might have perceived James I's new Oath of Allegiance as an appropriate political strategy offering English Catholics an opportunity to confess an allegiance to England's monarch that supersedes loyalty to the pope or to any Jesuit extremism like that of Guy Fawkes and company in the Gunpowder Plot. When Wray refers to the English regime's "laws" on 3 May 1641, he was promoting a unified support for the

---

[59] Patterson, *King James VI and I and the Reunion of Christendom*, 116–17.

[60] Dalton, *History of the Wrays of Glentworth*, 1:168, 171. Rigg concedes likewise that Wray's "presbyterianism was apparently untinged with republicanism" ("Wray," 994*b*).

English monarchy against the specter of a Catholic invasion, as well as against Laudian ecclesiastical sovereignty. In this context of the Army Plot, though, the popish threat is supported by the English monarch. Wray's rhetoric of king and country serves largely as a degree of exigent convention deployed at an historical moment of parliamentary aggression against both the throne and the episcopacy.[61] Crucially, the "National Oath" that Wray and company championed here differs from the Jacobean Oath of Allegiance beyond the external circumstances alone. Conrad Russell has noted that this Protestation of 1641 "identified loyalty with a [Protestant] cause, rather than with a person, and [it] authorized those who took it to resist any threat to that cause."[62] Wray's speech emphasizes that England's Protestant faith comes first, then its monarch, whose sovereignty and due glory will remain contingent on his relationship with the people, including the actions of royal executors like Strafford and Laud: "if the ballance of justice goe right, and his lawes be duly executed."[63] Here Wray's "if" resonates.

As the young John Wray of 1606 had labeled his Grand Tour a pilgrimage—a journey undertaken, he claims, for "[one's] owne betteringe, & his countries service"—so he calls himself a political "pilgrim" amid this later "journey" of faith within the Long Parliament.[64] Both pilgrim ventures in their own ways looked toward a patriotic purpose of godly reform. Here in 1641, Wray helped steer a new course for the form of his country's government. As for the irony of one Christian (Wray) aiming to kill another (Strafford) in the name of holy pilgrimage, we will leave that matter to God's judgment.

Northern Illinois University

---

[61] Cf. Russell, "Army Plot of 1641," 104–5; Peter Donald, *An Uncounselled King: Charles I and the Scottish Troubles, 1637–1641* (Cambridge, UK: Cambridge Univ. Press, 1990), 301–2.

[62] Russell, *Fall of the British Monarchies*, 295.

[63] Wray, *Eight Occasionall Speeches*, 12 (sig. B3*v*).

[64] Wray, *Pilgrims Iournall*, fol. 1*r*.9 (ed. Crowley, 197); Wray, *Eight Occasionall Speeches*, 12 (sig. B3*v*).

Book Reviews

James Shapiro, *The Year of Lear: Shakespeare in 1606*. New York: Simon & Schuster, 2015. Cloth, 367 pages.

Reviewed by Margaret Bockting, North Carolina Central University

The text, the writer, the audience, the context, the discursive field. Each scholar tends to privilege one or two elements and neglect the others. If you want examples of the "varieties of inconclusiveness" in *King Lear* and their presumed effects on an audience, turn to Stephen Booth's *King Lear, Macbeth, Indefinition, and Tragedy*.[1] But if you want to glimpse the varieties of inconclusiveness afflicting Jacobean England and their putative influence on Shakespeare's plays, then you'll want to peruse James Shapiro's *The Year of Lear*. Drawing on historical documents, biographies, histories, Shakespearean scholarship, and his own often very imaginative labors, Shapiro develops his argument that *King Lear, Macbeth, and Antony and Cleopatra* reflect the most important political and religious cleavages of the year 1606 and indeed of the Jacobean era itself. In his engaging prologue, for example, he avers that a court masque might mask but could not allay the problem of alienated nobles, who constituted but one instance of several emerging realignments in the kingdom. In the fourteen chapters that follow, he describes the social and political controversies that he argues troubled Shakespeare and his contemporaries.

Shapiro sees 1606 as a "cultural moment" in which the very definition of English identity was vehemently contested. Debates about the union of England and Scotland expressed deep uneasiness about political divisions and threats to national identity. Such cultural uneasiness is starkly re-inscribed by a play in which the

---

[1] Booth, *King Lear, Macbeth, Indefinition, and Tragedy* (New Haven, CT: Yale Univ. Press, 1983).

king parcels out his domains and France invades his kingdom. As Shapiro suggests, the political unconscious in *Lear* (and in *Macbeth*, which he covers in chapter 10) functions not as a fantasy of social conflict resolved, but as a nightmare of social antagonisms turned apocalyptic. He reinforces this reading of *Lear* by deftly examining the differences between Shakespeare's play and his principal source, *The True Chronicle History of King Leir*. Shapiro contends that the addition of the secondary plot about Edgar, the complication of motivations and consequences, the reiteration of "nothing" and other terms and prefixes signaling negation, and the deaths of Lear and Cordelia all contribute to the disconcerting effect of *King Lear*, observations consistent with Booth's earlier more purely textual reading of the play; Shapiro, however, contextualizes his aperçus in the Jacobeans' powerful dissatisfactions with their government's policies and their country's religious strife.

The fourth chapter focuses on documents from 1606 that reveal contemporary epistemological discussions: the contention between natural and supernatural explanations of various phenomena, including eclipses. He suggests that such conversations shaped the words of Gloucester and Edmund in the opening scenes of *King Lear*. In addition, he connects Anne Gunter's faked demonic possession to Edgar's assumption of the identity of Poor Tom. He argues that just as Gunter—supervised by her father—used Samuel Harsnett's *Declaration of Egregious Popish Impostures* as instructions in the art of performing possession, so Shakespeare relied on Harsnett in creating Edgar's disguise. Furthermore, he shows how the playwright's depiction of possession in 1606 differs from his earlier portrayals in *The Comedy of Errors* and *Twelfth Night*. Surprisingly, he does not comment on parallels and distinctions between Edgar's feigned possession and Hamlet's feigned madness or how their disguises relate to their struggles with abusive power.

Chapters 5, 6, and 7 describe the shock and after-shocks that accompanied the discovery of the Gunpowder Plot in November 1605. Imagining the devastating destruction that never happened, Shakespeare's contemporaries, Shapiro argues, became preoccupied with questions about the source of evil, questions that inform characterization and plot in both *King Lear* and *Macbeth*. These chapters narrate relevant events preceding and following Guy

Fawkes's arrest. After sketching the complicated figure of Lord Monteagle, who received a mysterious letter warning of an imminent terrorist attack, Shapiro details the investigation that led to Guy Fawkes's arrest and the "show trial" of the plotters (128). He emphasizes the government's efforts to control the meaning of the Gunpowder Plot, and describes the grisly executions of the conspirators, which included hanging, disemboweling, castration, and beheading. Observing that sermons preached after the Gunpowder Plot speak of evil's satanic origins, he infers that the offenders' executions served as a public exorcism. More importantly, he includes information about dissent, about those who questioned the official story, the preachers' representations, and the government's brutality. He acknowledges that it is difficult to determine "the extent to which contemporaries" doubted "the government's ever-changing version of events and its surprisingly harsh treatment of those implicated in the failed plot" (194); but his reference to a number of examples suggests that additional evidence may be discovered, and his brief analysis of *Volpone* demonstrates how to notice oblique counter-narratives. Ben Jonson's 1606 play, he says, locates evil "in men and women, not in imaginary devils who possess them," exposes trials as "merely good theater" (196), and indirectly criticizes the government's use of torture and extreme punishment. He also finds oblique dissent in Shakespeare's play, *Macbeth*, especially in its refusal "of easy explanations" for what motivates human cruelty.

The last six chapters of *Year of Lear* cover the extensive repercussions of the Gunpowder Plot, the controversies surrounding Catholic recusancy, and the growing disillusionment with King James. Shapiro links the discourses about these conditions to elements in *Macbeth* and *Antony and Cleopatra*. Contemporary descriptions of government actions, such as frantic preparations for attacks that didn't materialize, warrants, interrogations, and parades of prisoners, mirror the atmosphere that saturates *Macbeth*. Rumors of the decadence of the Jacobean court and of James's alleged callousness did nothing to allay contemporary anxieties. Shapiro finds evidence, in Sir John Harrington's "border-line treasonous" descriptions of events occurring during the Danish King's visit to England, that *Antony and Cleopatra* reflects contemporaries' "growing nostalgia" for the reign of Elizabeth (264–65).

The Year of Lear offers compelling connections between Shake-speare's plays and specific events experienced by the English in 1606. Scholars now have an opportunity to build on Shapiro's work by considering how the three plays' engagement with Jacobean politics affect how we interpret and perform these plays.

James Shapiro, *Shakespeare and the Jews: 20th Anniversary Edition.* New York: Columbia Univ. Press, 2016. Paperback, 317 pages.

Reviewed by Rachelle S. Gold, North Carolina Central University

James Shapiro's most provocative claim in *Shakespeare and the Jews* is that "the English turned to Jewish questions in order to answer English ones" (1). In the preface to his Twentieth Anniversary Edition, he asserts that his earlier edition does appear to have convinced his audience that there were, in fact, Jewish questions in Shakespeare's time, but he laments his lack of success in convincing scholars that Jews were threatening "precisely because they didn't outwardly appear all that different from Christians" (x). The broader significance of his thesis is that the Jewish questions provide "unusual insight into the cultural anxieties felt by English men and women at a time when their nation was experiencing extraordinary social, religious, and political turbulence" (1). At its core, Shapiro's book is a crisis-text; it stands in that long line of texts that try to root the irrefragable psychic disruptions of the early modern period in some kind of discernible social phenomena. Douglas Bush, for example, writing in 1945, attributed anxiety, what he called the melancholy strain in Tudor-Stuart literature, to an array of causes as diverse as indigestion, Puritanism, and the bubonic plague.[2] Lynn White added death and the devil to the list,[3] and Bill Bouwsma trumped

---

[2] Bush, Douglas, *English Literature in the Earlier Seventeenth Century 1600–1660* (Oxford: Clarendon Press, 1945).

[3] White, Lynn Jr., "Death and the Devil" in *The Darker Vision of the Renaissance: Beyond the Fields of Reason*, ed. Robert S. Kinsman (Berkeley: Univ. of California Press, 1974).

the devil with the ineluctable movement of time.[4] Stephen Orgel[5] returned our attention to indigestion, or potential indigestion, with his essay, "Shakespeare and the Cannibals," and Mark Brietenburg indicted patriarchal privilege itself with his famous quip that "'anxious masculinity' is redundant."[6] And Shapiro adds Jews to the list of anxiety causing phenomena.

We know, of course, that in the period before the expulsion of the Jews in 1290, Jews were a source of anxiety, and that this anxiety was codified in texts such as the *Leges Edwardi Confessoris* dating from around 1120:

> Be it known that since [*sic*] all Jews, wherever they are in the kingdom, *ought to be under the liege guardianship and protection of the king*; nor can any one of them subject himself to any wealthy man without the license of the king, since the Jews and all their possessions are the king's. But if anyone shall have detained them or their money, the king can demand it as his own property, if he can and wishes to.

This snippet from the *Leges*, discussed in Kevin Streit's "The Expansion of the English Jewish Community in the Reign of King Stephen" (1993) contains a number of noteworthy features not the least of which is the phrase "wherever they are," which suggests that the framers of the law were exercised not only by the presence of Jews and their potential economic impact, but by their inability to know exactly where these Jews were lurking in the kingdom. During Shakespeare's lifetime, Portuguese Marranos notwithstanding, both Jews and the laws constraining them are hard to find in England. From 1570 onward, anxieties and the institutional sanctions in which they eventuated increasingly focused on Catholic recusants. As Conrad Russel chronicles in *The Crisis of Parliaments*:

---

[4] Bouwsma, William J., "Anxiety and the Formation of Early Modern Culture," in *A Usable Past: Essays in European Cultural History* (Berkeley: Univ. of California Press, 1990), 157–89.

[5] Orgel, Stephen, "Shakespeare and the Cannibals" in *Cannibals, Witches, and Divorce: Estranging the Renaissance,* ed. Marjorie Garber (Baltimore, MD: The Johns Hopkins Univ. Press, 1987), 40–66.

[6] Breitenberg, Mark, *Anxious Masculinity in Early Modern England* (Cambridge, UK: Cambridge Univ. Press, 1996).

English History 1509–1660, recusants were fined, forcibly re-educated, compelled to "forfeit two-thirds of their estate for failing to attend church," (208), fired from jobs, excluded from the militia, and priests were "denounced for their delight in blood" (208). Despite some legal cases that unequivocally prove that there were a few Jews in England after 1290 and before their readmission in 1656, Shapiro's evidence is largely anecdotal. Had Jews been a source of anxiety equal to Catholics or Puritans, one would expect to find more than anecdotes documenting that fact. Indeed, in *The Year of Lear: Shakespeare in 1606* (2015), Shapiro himself affirms that "The fallout from the Gunpowder Plot led to a heightened anxiety over Jesuitical equivocation" (9); his claim underscores the range of possible sources of English cultural anxiety. While Jews, Jesuits, Turks, and Moors, were vilified as needed both on the stage and on the page, it is hard to see them as the font of the cultural disturbance that gripped Shakespeare's England.

Meticulously researched, Shapiro's book is particularly useful for the vivid way in which it depicts how Jews were treated and artistically represented in the period. The cover features a 1611 illustration from a travel book, *Coryats Crudities*. The image depicts a bearded reportedly Jewish man chasing Thomas Coryate, the travel book's author, with a knife, as Coryate flees fearfully, his rear-facing gaze fixed on his menacing would-be assailant. Ironically, Coryate had traveled to the Venetian ghetto to convert Jews, escaping after he discovered that proselytizing had its dangers. Minor poets of the time such as Laurence Whitaker in his commendatory poems written for the *Crudities* mocked Coryate's apparent anxiety, punning that the Jew planned only to circumcise him, not kill him (115). "Jewish crimes" such as forced circumcision and murder were rooted in the cultural myth that in order to avoid expulsion in 1290, Jews masqueraded as Christians, and resentful at having to worship secretly, retaliated by kidnapping, circumcising, and then murdering gentile babies or men; *Shakespeare and the Jews* is replete with examples that underscore (For instance, Queen Elizabeth was rumored to be a Jew.) the pervasiveness of such cultural fantasies.

Except for a few isolated incidents of fanatical Jews and radical Puritans, Shapiro avers, "there is no evidence that circumcisions took place in early modern England" (115). Shapiro argues that the "real" anxieties coalesced around what qualities define who and what a Jew is, what Jews look like, and how they can deceive unsuspecting Christians. Despite the fact that *Shakespeare and the Jews* includes some archival data and miscellaneous legal cases, Shapiro's goal to convince readers of why Jews "threatened to contaminate the English body and body politic" (225) falls, in terms of evidence, somewhat short of the mark. With provocative chapter titles such as "False Jews and Counterfeit Christians," "'The Jewish Crime,'" "'The Pound of Flesh,'" and "The Hebrew Will Turn Christian," Shapiro situates his work at the juncture between defensive historical research and a defense of the Bard's play with Shylock at the center.

Shapiro is most successful in illustrating how Jews had been mistreated in England after the majority of them had been expelled. The unhappy remnant were forced to wear certain clothing that distinguished them and were, in some cases, pilloried, tattooed, forced to eat pork, and even executed (13–16). He also emphasizes that Jewish otherness was "exaggerated and at times simply invented: other people were deemed un-English in the way that they looked, prayed, ate, smelled, dressed, walked, and talked . . . The early modern Jew confounded those who sought more precise definitions in terms suited to emerging notions of nationhood and race" (5). No one questions that Jews as a people resisted simple classification since they were physically identical to Christians, but the degree to which Jews became a significant tributary for the river of cultural anxiety in the period remains highly speculative.

Shapiro concludes that shifts in cultural identity mark the early modern period and that one such shift began with the English Reformation and ended when the Jewish Naturalization Act passed in 1753, which created "a change in English attitudes toward Jews and Jewishness as the opposition of Christian and Jew was slowly overtaken by that of Englishman and Jew" (225). In *The Year of Lear*, Shapiro insists that "the theatre was the one place where rich and poor could congregate and see enacted through old or made-up stories, a refracted image of their own desires and anxieties" (11). All viewers of the 1611 cover illustration of *Shakespeare and the Jews* project their own apprehensions upon the image as a "made-up story" because no distinguishing features, clothing, or religious symbols identify the knife-wielder as a Jew; in fact, both men are bearded, dressed in flowing garments, and wear hats. Perhaps we can read the image paradiastolically; instead of wanting to stab or circumcise Coryate, a foreign invader, the alleged Jew might have been defending his segregated city, the ghetto in Venice that represented the very real anti-Semitism that is at the heart of Shapiro's interest in representations of Shylock. The abiding value of *Shakespeare and the Jews* is that it allows us to re-imagine its cover image as a portrait of a man protecting his culture, religion, and his family rather than as an image of greed, retribution, or revenge.